Lost to Darkness;

Enlightened by Grace

Laura Gabriela

Lost to Darkness; Enlightened by Grace

Printed in the United States of America.

ISBN-13: 978-1-7347356-7-3

Cover photo credit: Pablo Korona

Marshmallow's Publishing

Rockford, Illinois

MARSHMALLOW'S

PUBLISHING

Warning

The contents of this book may be triggering to some readers as it contains explicit content pertaining to suicide and abuse.

Dedication

I'd like to first and foremost thank God for moving mountains for me to be able to share my story.

"For I know the plans I have for you,"
declares the Lord, "plans to prosper you and
not to harm you, plans to give you hope and
a future" (Jeremiah 29:11 NIV).

I want to dedicate this book to my three babies: Kaitlynn, Zachary, and Lincoln. You are the strength that drives me to be the better version of myself. Kait and Lincoln, always remember that you can do anything that you put your mind to. There are no limits to your potential. Always strive for your dreams and know that I love you with everything that I am. To my Zachary, I promise that your story will live on until my last breath. Through you, I will do whatever I can to create awareness and save others. I want the three of you to know that you're my world and I will always strive to make you proud.

To Jonathan: Thank you for encouraging me to write this book and always sticking by me through my darkest moments. You have been my greatest cheerleader! Always going along with all my entrepreneurial ideas, but most of all, you have been my rock and my greatest supporter. I am forever grateful for your love, encouragement, and for the fact that you've shown me the Light and have taught me more than I could have ever imagined. You are my strength in Christ.

To Haile, Liam, Anthony, and Adrian: I am super blessed to call you family, and I'm grateful that you're a part of my life.

To all my family, my mother, my stepdad, my aunt, uncles, my siblings, cousins, the Kane's, and Sue: I am grateful for all the love and support you've given me. Thank you for never giving up on me and always encouraging me to keep moving forward.

To my grandmother, Aurora: You raised us kids to be amazing people, and I am grateful for you instilling in me how important it is to love people unconditionally, and that hard work pays off. I love you, Grandma.

To my friends: Thank you for being supportive- I am grateful for you.

To all of the mothers I've met along the way who have lost a child: We share the same pain, and we lift each other up. I am forever grateful for the tears we've shed together. This book is for you and your beautiful children.

To all of you dealing with domestic violence: Please know that you're strong enough to walk away even when it seems impossible. To the ones struggling with mental illness, it is okay to not be okay, never stay quiet, talk about it, there is help! To the ones taking the time to read my book, my prayer is that you can find hope and inspiration, and if there is something relatable to you in my story, that you know that you're not alone, you can overcome the pain and persevere. Thank you from the bottom of my heart for your support.

A special thanks to Mr. E. Eklund, Mr. Cotton-Smidt, Mr. New, Mr. Sholl, Mrs. Benson & Rich Foster. Thank you for always being kind to my children and encouraging them through good and bad. I will forever be grateful for the support you gave us.

To Nicole and Peter: Thank you from the bottom of my heart! Super grateful for the two of you helping me make this book happen.

Thank you Troy Thompson for the amazing promo video and to Pablo Korona for the incredible cover picture.

Contents

Chapter 1

Once upon a Time in Mexico…

Picture this: a young girl is riding her pink and white bicycle down the street. Her long brown hair is waving in the wind behind her. The smile on her light brown face is stretching ear to ear. She's on her way to Grandma's house. What in the world could be better than visiting the person that showers you with love and sweets?

Fast forward thirty years down the road, and the same young girl is now a woman. Her long brown hair is shorter, with a few white and gray strands throughout it. She's curled into the fetal position on the floor in the corner of her bedroom, hugging a pillow. The pillow she's buried her face in is muffling the agonizing sobs. How in the world did she arrive at this moment?

There's a saying that was made famous by Tom Hanks in the movie *Forrest Gump*, "Life was like a box of chocolates, you never know what you're gonna get."

For most of us, sayings like this have a tendency to go in one ear and out the other. We really don't think too much on the, "you never know what you're gonna get." Some of us hear that and think, "That's for people who don't make plans for their lives. I'm ready for whatever comes my way."

Most of us think we're invincible against the "never know what you're gonna get" life might throw our way. That is, until we actually go through the unexpected and unknown. A close relative passes away suddenly and unexpectedly, creating feelings of deep sadness and abandonment. The places you said you'd never end up are now listed as your permanent residence. The picture-perfect family you thought you had shatters in divorce court.

Do we adequately plan for these situations? Of course not! Nobody ever falls in love with their high school sweetheart, and in the back of their mind thinks, "Here's my plan in case this goes south, and we get a divorce." For the most part, the majority of us plan for the good, whatever we think "the good" might be. Sometimes it's an unattainable illusion that we have set for ourselves based on movies we've watched or books we've read. Other times it is just hopeful thinking. Maybe our home life isn't that great, so we hope for something better. Whichever the case may be, none of us *plan* to have our plans interrupted.

This story is about a bunch of interrupted plans. I'm that woman who muffled sobs in the pillow so my children wouldn't hear my broken-down overwhelmed cry of defeat.

It wasn't always that way. I hadn't planned for things to go that way, but like Forrest said, "You never know what you're gonna get."

My childhood was not exactly what you would call normal. My mother was only 15 when she gave birth to me, and my father was never in my life. I'm sure as you can imagine, a child raising a baby wasn't exactly ideal. I was born in Mexico City, and lived in a 3-bedroom condo with my mother, grandmother, grandfather, aunt, and two uncles.

Despite her old age now, I will always remember my grandmother as she looked back then. She had long straight black hair that stretched down below her waist line. Every single morning, she would wake up early and put on makeup. She would stand in front of the mirror by the bathroom sink, and I'd watch her putting on her eyeliner and admiring how beautiful she was. She looked like Morticia Addams from *The Addams Family*.

Our family owned a pharmacy 45 minutes away from our house. Most days, I would ride with my grandmother to our pharmacy in her forest green Monte Carlo. As I laid on the green suede backseat curled up in a Smurfs blanket, she would sing songs of worship and prayer to me. The best part of the ride was *my* sunflower. About halfway to the pharmacy, I would sit up and look out the window. There were huge buildings all around us, and in front of one of those buildings stood a beautiful sunflower. *My* sunflower. I loved watching it turn to face the sun. Every day, I would ask my grandmother if we were almost to *my* sunflower because seeing that beautiful bright and yellow sunflower would cause everything else to blur into the background and disappear into oblivion. Seeing *my* sunflower gave me so much peace and joy.

My grandfather was a lawyer, so he was gone most of the time. When he was home, I would run around the house pretending I was a puppy dog, while he lounged in his chair with a green and grey blanket. I have beautiful memories of my childhood from back then. Sadly, when I was 4 years old, he passed away, and everything changed. As a lawyer, my grandfather made good money. Now that he was gone, my grandmother, only 50 years old at the time of his death, was left with her hands full.

She had let the help at the pharmacy go, which meant she would be there all day long. We'd leave the house at six in the morning and wouldn't get back home until ten at night. She enrolled me at a school near the pharmacy for a little while, but eventually couldn't afford to keep me there. Raising myself and her four teenagers wasn't an easy task. She even had a side hustle delivering bread and muffins to people on the weekends when she wasn't working at the pharmacy. I would always get that one warm and moist freshly baked banana nut muffin on our way to her deliveries. It was delicious and something that I'd look forward to.

My mom was young and trying to figure out her own life. We didn't spend much time together. So, when I wasn't going to the pharmacy with my grandmother, I was at home hanging out with a bunch of teenagers. It never seemed odd, because for me, I was just hanging out with my aunt and uncles along with their crazy teenage friends. There was a lot of drinking and partying going on since there wasn't any adult supervision, so I probably saw things little kids shouldn't see. They always ensured that I was safe and taken care of, though, so I loved all of it. I was closest to my aunt, Angelina, attached to her hip, some might say. She didn't mind. She would drag me along all over town with her and her friends. Then one day, my world changed forever once again. My aunt said she was leaving for the United States. My mom followed shortly after, leaving me in Mexico with my grandmother and my uncles. It was a bittersweet moment. My aunt/best friend was gone, but I still had my uncles, who, by the way, were the greatest friends a girl could ever have!

We would listen to 80s punk rock, Spanish rock, and just plain rock n' roll music all the time. We'd dance around the house while one of them would play the drums. They were so good about walking me to and from school; pretty much taking care of me while my poor grandmother slaved away at the pharmacy. Every Sunday, my grandmother would leave me an allowance on her bedroom dresser; 5 pesos to be exact! I would ride my pink and white bicycle to the building next door, where a lady had a candy store. I loved going there because it made me feel like such an independent kid. I would ride my bike through this tiny garden full of flowers. It had a little stone walkway that led up to a small window, where a lady would open her window and sell me candy. I would peak through that window, and there were all kinds of goodies! All the sweet flavors of Mexico through a tiny window.

Then, once again, my life changed drastically. When I was nine years old, my mother came back to Mexico. She told my grandmother that she was getting married and wanted to take me to the US with her. A few months later, that's exactly what happened. I said bye to Mexico and moved to sunny Florida. I wasn't sure how I felt about living with my mom; up to this point, my grandmother had been that mother figure to me. But I was super excited that I would get to see my aunt, Angelina.

Chapter 2

Sunshine and Skaters

To say that life in Florida was different than Mexico would be a bit of an understatement. In Mexico, I thrived in school. I was confident and used to being the center of attention. But in Florida, I was the oddball out. I started 4th grade at the local elementary school, not knowing any English at all. I'm not sure that I can adequately describe how scary it was for a nine-year-old to be surrounded by a school full of people you can't communicate with. Kids would laugh at me for the way I pronounced and enunciated words.

I'm sure this could have suffered a major setback in my life if I had not been so determined to move forward. I was going to learn English, and since music was my escape, every single night, I would take my Walkman and listen to Green Day for hours! I would rewind songs and write down what I thought the lyrics were saying over and over. Then I began singing along with the songs while reading through the lyrics I had written down. Eventually, I was singing the popular Green Day songs without an accent. For anyone reading this that may be struggling with language barriers, just keep in mind, Green Day taught me English- haha.

Things began getting better at school, but my home life was plummeting. I didn't really get along with my mom's husband, so the summer before my 8th grade year, I moved in with my aunt and uncle. She was the same aunt I had grown up with in Mexico. We lived in a cute neighborhood in Davenport, Florida. Literally in the middle of orange groves. There were a ton of kids in the neighborhood. Somehow, since I was the new girl in town, I was instantly popular and had TONS of friends. All the kids on our block were super close. We hung out all summer, played games, like Capture the Flag and 7 Minutes in Heaven. I got my very first kiss from the boy who lived directly across the street from me. Little did I know, he and I would become inseparable for years.

I started 8th grade hanging out with the "head bangers and skaters". On my first day of 8th grade, I wore JNCO bell bottom jeans, and I thought I was hot stuff. Every day right after the last class, there was a bus that stopped at the middle school from the high school to pick up kids. There was a tall high schooler skater kid that would get off the bus with long blonde hair who all the girls would swarm around. He was a few years older than me, and honestly, I didn't understand what all the girls saw in this skinny kid. I didn't see the appeal; years later, he would turn out to be my husband. But let's not jump ahead too far just yet.

Moving in with my aunt and uncle had been the absolute best thing that ever happened to me. I didn't have many rules at home. That may sound like an eighth grader's dream situation, but honestly, it came about through trust. My aunt and uncle trusted me to do the right thing- come home at dark, get my homework done, and just make the right choices by using common sense. Seems like a lot of faith to put in a teenager, but I think the reason it worked was because my uncle never really talked to me like I was a kid. He always instilled the importance of getting an education, and used physiological analogies to paint pictures in my mind of what a successful life was supposed to look like.

I finally felt like I belonged to a family. My aunt and uncle had three kids of their own, but they never once made me feel like an outsider. My aunt and uncle worked a lot, so I would be home babysitting my little cousins. The neighborhood kids would often come help me babysit, even when no one was supposed to be around. It was a great time in my life.

When I was fourteen, my uncle's mother came to live with us. She had been battling cancer for many years, so moving in with us would provide extra help in case she needed it. At first, she was grandma to my cousins, but it didn't take long before she became my best friend- Grandma Lynn. She taught me so much about life and relationships. She even taught me how to drive. She was someone that I could confide in, truly, for the first time in my life.

Most nights while my aunt and uncle were sleeping in their room, we would stay up all night, talking about life, listening to oldies, or watching professional ice skating on TV. I would watch her bobby pin small pink curlers in her hair while she cracked open the window and blew cigarette smoke outside. She would tell me

9

love stories of her past, and share things with me about her life to teach me, "what not to do." She lived with a lot of regret when it came to her relationships, but truthfully, she was my hero because despite everything she ever went through, she persevered.

For this reason, she was the one I talked to when I fell in love with the boy across the street. He was a handsome blue-eyed football player. He was a big class clown, but we could laugh for hours. We would break up and get back together; he was my high school sweetheart. One of my greatest memories is him showing up to Grandma Lynn's window with a boom box, serenading me in the middle of the night to the latest remix of Bohemian Rhapsody and the corniest Boys to Men songs in existence. Grandma Lynn and I were beyond entertained.

On Thanksgiving morning, Grandma Lynn would wake up at 6am to put the turkey in the oven. She would slave away in the kitchen all morning, making mashed potatoes, yam casserole, green bean casserole, and all kinds of other delicious foods. She would always make sure that Thanksgiving dinner was done no later than 1:00 PM, so we could eat the dinner, watch football, and snack on leftovers all day. She was a huge football fan. One year, she screamed at Dan Marino in excitement to get that touchdown! She'd do a goofy dance with her fingers pointing up and her tongue sticking out.

She was the constant in my life. As her health declined, since my aunt and uncle worked so much, I became the one helping take care of her. The cancer got so bad that her lungs were filling up with fluid constantly. Eventually, they had to put permanent draining tubes in each lung. Nurses would visit the house daily to drain her lungs. The nursing staff was inconsistent, and it seemed like there was a new nurse each visit. I hated seeing them unintentionally hurt her by having to try to figure out how to get the draining tubes to drain. So, eventually, I just took over and had them watch me do it so that I didn't have to watch a different nurse struggle with the tubes and hurt her in the process.

When I was 16, I got a full-time job during the summer. I played volleyball, had really good grades, and was also super active in JROTC (Junior Reserve Officers Training Court). If you're not familiar with the program, it is a federal program sponsored by the United States Armed Forces. Some of the goals for the program are to develop citizenship and patriotism within the cadets enrolled. It is also very helpful with instilling an appreciation for physical fitness and team building skills. I got to compete with the drill team, that was a fun experience. This program had a major role in my planning my future. I planned to join the Army and attend college after I graduated. I had a lot of plans, but one night changed all of that.

Chapter 3

You Never Know What You're Gonna Get

I got off work and decided not to go straight home. Instead, I went to hang out across the street with my boyfriend. I felt scared. There was something keeping me from going home, but I don't even know why I was scared. I suppose I thought I would get in trouble for coming home at 2 AM. It wasn't the norm for me to stay out that late, so perhaps it wouldn't have been so bad, but being a teenager, I didn't have that rational reasoning going through my mind. Finally, I worked up the nerve to cross the street and walk into the house. I went straight to Grandma Lynn's bedroom to check on her, but instead of her being asleep in bed, she was lying on the floor- dead! Her stiffened body and her vividly lifeless blue eyes filled my shocked body with sadness. Her oxygen tube, which she was wearing for months, was lying next to her face. I stood in shock, staring at her as if I was having a bad dream. Suddenly, I got a burst of energy, ran into my aunt and uncle's room, and screamed, "Grandma's dead."

My uncle jumped out of bed and frantically ran across the house towards her room in disbelief. We both were filled with devastation over our loss, but also knew her battle with cancer was finally over, and she was free from the pain.

After she died, my life began to change drastically. Here I was, starting my senior year of high school, my high school sweetheart was sent away to live in another state, and my best friend, Grandma Lynn, was dead. This was not at all how I had planned for things to go. Getting good grades and attending every class no longer seemed important. I made some new friends and got involved in the party scene. Even though I started letting things slip, the values that my uncle had instilled in me kept invisible boundaries in place. This might be okay, but you don't cross that line kind of thing.

The boundary lines became a little blurred the first time I tried ecstasy. My friend asked me to drive him to his cousin's house. As soon as we entered the house, his cousin looked at me and said, "Stick out your tongue."

Being the naïve teen that I was, I stuck out my tongue, and he stuck a pill to it. "Chew it."

I did, and it was the absolute most horrible taste in the world. He looked at my friend and said "You've got 25 minutes to get to your destination, she's officially taken a triple stack dolphin."

My friend said, "Noooo, she's never done it before."

At that moment, I thought, "Oh shit! What did I do?"

We made it back to his house, where he put out lawn chairs in his garage and put these big headphones on my head, turned on a strobe light that changed colors, and well...I chose to do ecstasy every weekend after that. That was March before graduation. Drugs had never been something that I could see myself doing, but this helped to numb the pain. I didn't have to think about losing Grandma Lynn or my boyfriend moving away. I didn't have to worry about keeping up my grades, what my aunt and uncle were thinking, what my plans for the future should be. In those moments, I wouldn't have to think about anything, and that is what made it perfect.

Then one night in April, I was at a party with friends. We wanted to do some ecstasy, but the person said they only had cocaine. Even with all the blurred boundaries of what was now right and wrong, doing cocaine was not at all on my to-do list. In fact, it was still on my "just don't go there" list. I said that I knew somewhere we could get some ecstasy, but my friend wanted to stay and try it. So, I left the party with two guys I had just met that night.

We found some ecstasy and were flying high all night. The next morning, we were definitely not making it to school. I had zero sleep, so I let one of the guys drive my car back from the dealer's house to the town he lived in. I never thought that one simple choice could end up being so life-altering. As we were driving, I had dozed off in the passenger's seat; and suddenly, I woke up from a dead sleep, and I screamed at him and yanked the steering

15

wheel to the right, just before we hit a telephone pole going 50 miles an hour. The kid driving was looking down, lighting a cigarette, so he didn't notice that we were headed for the pole head on. Had I not grabbed the wheel, the car would have smashed into the telephone pole entirely on the passenger's side, my side of the car. I honestly don't think I'd even be here today if that would have happened. But because I jerked the wheel, it ended up hitting the pole straight on. The entire front of my '92 white Chrysler Lebaron was completely wrapped around the pole. The kid riding in the backseat didn't have a seatbelt on, he was laying across the backseat sleeping, so he ended up flying to the front and hitting his head on the windshield, getting scalped. He was air-flown to a trauma hospital where he luckily was able to have reconstructive plastic surgery, and more importantly, survive.

I had lost consciousness, but I remembered some civilians pulling us from the car. Two elderly women stayed with me and prayed with me. They kept telling me that I was going to be ok. They did this over and over until the paramedics showed up. I asked the paramedics where the two ladies were that had been praying with me, but they kept telling me there weren't any ladies there. To this day, I am convinced that they must have been angels sent by Grandma Lynn to watch over me and comfort me until the paramedics showed up.

My aunt Angelina showed up to the hospital. My legs had been smashed up pretty badly, but luckily, I only suffered a fracture to my right ankle. I was released from the hospital, and the drive home with my aunt was pretty silent for the most part. She was definitely upset with me as I should have been in school. When I got home, I went straight to bed, and while I lay there, my uncle came in to my room. "Well...I'm glad you're alive." That was all he said, and then walked out of the room. If you're not a parent, you might write him off as a cruel-hearted person. But honestly, that was probably the only thought he had to hold onto at the time. I'm sure they were both wondering what in the world had happened to the good girl they had raised.

As if fracturing my ankle, totaling my car, and facing the disappointment from my aunt and uncle wasn't bad enough, I was the only one in the car who was 18 and had a driver's license. That meant the huge lawsuit that was filed was all against me and my parents. The boy that had been driving was a police officer's son, so he literally walked away from it all with only a scratch on his arm. The whole ordeal destroyed my driving record.

I had already passed all my paper and physical exams to join the military right after graduation. Those plans had now been shattered with my ankle in the car accident. That wouldn't be happening. I ditched way too many classes to even care about attending college anymore. I was amazed that I even had enough credits to graduate come May.

Eighteen years old and all my plans for life were now gone.

Chapter 4

One Bad Decision + One Bad Decision = One More Bad Decision

I was eighteen, and my best friend at the time asked me to give her a ride to see a friend. Apparently, this *friend* had been arrested at the age of seventeen for burglarizing rental homes. He and his friends would steal credit cards, buy money orders with them, then ditch the credit cards. Eventually, they got caught, and this guy served a couple of years in prison since he was tried as an adult. I never knew anyone who had been to jail, not personally. After all, I was raised to live my life honestly and get an education. Knowing this guy had been in jail set my mind with a prejudgment that this guy was most definitely no good to be around. But since it seemed so important to my friend, I decided to drive her the few miles down the road to meet up with him.

We pulled into a trailer park and rolled up to a white-double wide trailer with cute little plants all around. There was a small patio area with stairs that led to the front door and had hanging plants all around the top of it. As we stopped in front of the trailer, my friend said, "This is it!" as she sprung from the car with excitement. Walking down the patio stairs towards the car, I see this super tall, slender guy with brown hair and a charming smile.

He was a very well-groomed, clean-cut guy. I had to do a double-take because it was that blonde, long-haired skater boy from the high school bus that all the girls would go gaga over when I was in middle school. He walked up to my friend and picked her up in a bear hug; they were genuinely happy to see each other. I thought, "Damn, he is fine." Not sure what had changed since middle school, but I liked how he looked now.

Then, to my surprise, he walked around to my side of the car, opened my car door, and in this deep voice, said, "Hey Laura, how have you been?" as if he'd known me forever.

He said that he had heard so much about me from my friend. Which I thought was kind of odd since I hadn't heard very much about him at all. The most I heard from my friend was that she had received a few letters from this guy in prison. I always blew it off and didn't listen, thinking he was probably a loser. I got out of the car and he gave me a huge hug. I wasn't really sure what to think of this guy.

The three of us were constantly hanging out. We'd go to bonfires and parties together. I was always the third wheel, but since she was one of the only friends I had, I didn't think much about it. During the several months that the three of us had been hanging out, she started seeing another guy on the side. She would always ask me to cover for her. She would typically plan stuff on Wednesday nights because her mom would go to church on Wednesdays. We'd have plans for the three of us to hang out somewhere or do something, then she would say that her mom was making her go to church. In reality, she'd be seeing the other guy.

I would have been perfectly content never hanging out with him, but she always had a way of guilting me into spending time with him to cover for her. If I was with him, then he would buy the story of her being at church with her mom. He wouldn't try to go look for her because he knew we were pretty inseparable other than when she was at "church," and so he wouldn't catch her cheating on him. It was an awful mess, and one day all those dirty secrets were exposed. Unfortunately, I was the one to expose them.

Once again, she went to hang out with her other boyfriend, and I was told to cover for her. We were hanging out with some friends down the street from his trailer. We decided to take some ecstasy. Ecstasy is like a truth serum, at least it was for me. So, it was an absolute awful drug to take when you're with your best friend's boyfriend, and she's cheating on him. We were getting very touchy-feely, and before you know it, I'm telling him that he deserves so much better. I proceed to tell him that she's been cheating on him. One thing led to another after that, and we ended up having sex that night.

Talk about feeling like a terrible friend. The next morning, sober, I tried to talk to her to tell her what happened, but it was too late. I lost my best friend, and in one night, just like that, I fell madly in love with her boyfriend.

He and I soon became inseparable. His mother talked us into buying ourselves a small single-wide trailer. My aunt and uncle were furious! This was not the life they envisioned for me, but most teenagers think "I knew best," and did it anyway. I threw away all my plans of going to college and joining the army for this guy and the tiny little home we were buying. You might be wondering what on earth was I thinking. I wasn't thinking at all, I was simply *in love*!

It was literally the smallest...tiniest...little place. When you entered the front door, you'd find yourself in the living room. It was only big enough for a couch. To the right of the living room, there was a tiny bedroom, and to the left of the living room was the kitchen with the washer and dryer in it next to a short hallway. To the far back of the hallway, there was another bedroom barely big enough to cram a queen size bed and dresser. The bathroom was more like a half bathroom with a tiny shower. The biggest space in the whole house was the screened-in porch that stretched across the front. That was truthfully about as big as the living room and kitchen put together.

When I got those keys, at eighteen, I felt like the happiest girl on earth.

He was always attentive, always super loving, and affectionate. I worked as a cashier making $6.50 an hour, and he was a stock boy at the same grocery store, working graveyard, making $10.00. Within three months of living together, we planned our entire lives! We knew we wanted to have two kids- a boy and a girl. We wanted to get married, and we just had life figured out. What eighteen-year-old doesn't have it figured out in their eyes?

Chapter 5-

Blinded by Love

As far back as I can remember, I always prayed for a beautiful family of my own. I would kneel in front of my bed at night, and pray for a tall, skinny, brown-haired beautiful daughter with crimson red lips. And since I idolized the show *Saved by the Bell* and had a huge crush on Zachary Morris, I also prayed for a handsome son named Zachary. That was my plan- a beautiful daughter, a beautiful son named Zachary. I suppose I should have spent a bit more time planning what a marriage would look like as well.

Six months after living together, my boyfriend asked me if I wanted a baby. Of course, I said yes, I had dreamed of being a mother my entire life. A month after trying, we found out we were having our first child, and we were jumping for joy. His parents were excited for us, but didn't want us to have a baby out of wedlock.

One day, when I got home from work, he got down on one knee, in our tiny kitchen, and proposed to me. I was the happiest girl in the world. My mom had taken me from my family in Mexico. Then after not fitting well with her and her husband I went to live with my aunt and uncle. They always treated me like one of their own children, but my decisions over the past few years had caused a strain on our relationship. Now I was about to have *my* very own family. It was like a dream come true!

Even though things had been a little rocky between us, I was excited to go home and give my aunt and uncle the news. My sweet grandmother from Mexico was now living with them, so I was even more excited to deliver the news.

I sat down in my aunt's kitchen to tell her and *Abuelita*, "I have some news. I'm having a baby, and I'm going to get married."

In the meantime, my now fiancé tried being somewhat traditional. Although he had already proposed, he asked my uncle for my hand in marriage. I'm not sure how that conversation went down between the two of them, I never got the details. But what I can tell you is this, everyone in my family was outraged, and although they wanted to be supportive, they did tell me over and over not to marry him. They kept telling me that just because I was having a baby, it didn't mean I had to marry him.

I probably should have taken a moment to listen to these people that had loved me for the past eighteen years. They knew the person that I had been and the potential of what I could become. Instead, I began planning our "dream" wedding, and didn't really speak to them.

I wanted to get married by the ocean, so we planned the ceremony a couple hours away. I was six months pregnant. His aunt up North had picked out and bought my wedding dress, which was a bit big on me. I was grateful, but I didn't even get to look for my own wedding dress. We rented this pretty beatdown motel reception hall that had windows facing the ocean. We would have finger foods and a boom box to play the music. His mother had asked the pastor of her church to marry us. It was going to be simple, but beautiful.

But on the day of our wedding, in ninety-eight-degree weather, the air conditioner at the reception hall broke. It was not at all beautiful. I was really, really upset. The whole point of being married on the beach was defeated when his mother set up the ceremony inside that terribly hot room. We weren't supposed to get married in the reception hall. We were supposed to get married on the beach with the beautiful oceanfront behind us.

That didn't happen.

That should have been a clear indication from the beginning. It was all going to be doom and gloom from there. But, of course, it wasn't because I was blinded by love.

All of his childhood friends were there, and all of them were in the parking lot hot-boxing their cars, smoking pot. I knew they were all potheads, including him, so their actions didn't surprise me. But my family was pretty straight and narrow, drugs were never a thing, and I had asked all of those friends prior to the wedding not to bring any drugs. I told my new husband that I felt super disrespected and asked him to tell all his friends to leave.

From that day forward, none of his friends liked me.

What should have been remembered as a fairy-tale dream with an oceanfront wedding was replaced with a mother-in-law planned hot-boxing mess. It wasn't at all something to be remembered, but it was just one day, right? It was now just the two of us, and everything was alright.

I loved the fact that I was now his wife. Despite his friends not liking me, he always brought me around them and always demanded them to respect me. At that point in our lives, he was my world. My family and I had a very strained relationship, and for years, my uncle and I didn't even speak. I really had no friends. My husband, his friends, and his family were the only people I hung out with. That never bothered me, though, because he treated me like a queen.

The queen-like treatment included many different things, but one of my favorite memories was the Valentine's Day before we got married. He came home with something in his shirt, and when he lifted his shirt up, all you could see was a huge red fluff ball. He brought home our very first puppy. It was a full-blooded Chow Chow pup. Unfortunately, this dog decided to destroy the trailer the day we brought our daughter home from the hospital, so we decided to get rid of it to ensure our baby would be safe.

I worked evenings, and he worked the graveyard shift. Then one day, he came home telling me he had met some people who worked in construction. He was pretty sure they could get him a job. He was going to do this for his family- our little family. He went from making $10 an hour to $15 an hour operating heavy machinery.

We turned the tiny back bedroom into a Disney princess nursery. Then, on September 11, 2002, we brought our daughter Kaitlynn into the world. She looked like a little Eskimo with a head full of pitch-black hair. She had the softest and fairest skin. Her eyes were as black as the night. Our world could not be more perfect. We had the type of love that people envied. Truthfully, life was amazing, and that little girl became the center of our world. We lived in the trailer until Kait was almost two years old.

Chapter 6-

My Own Little Fairy
Tale...Nightmare

During the first few years of our marriage, all the "little" things I had once ignored in our relationship began growing into much bigger issues. Although we had both agreed not to do drugs once Kaitlynn was born, they continued to find their way into our lives. I had never been raised around drugs, and even weed was a bit taboo in my mind because of my straight upbringing. So, cutting off drugs didn't seem to come with much of a challenge for me. Whereas with his upbringing, it was acceptable to be high all the time.

So, it probably shouldn't have surprised me when he would sneak off to smoke pot with his friends and come home high. But every time it happened, we'd get into heated arguments. I figured it was just disagreement normal to every married couple because we would always make up.

There were even a few times that we had his parents babysit overnight, and he talked me into doing ecstasy with him "for old time's sake." Thankfully, one of the times I had a bad experience where my hands curved up like a crippled person. All I could think about was being like that for the rest of my life and not being around for my family. That was the end of drugs for me.

Part of our plans included having our second child no more than twenty-four months apart from the first. So, with Kaitlynn being almost two, it was no surprise to us that our baby boy Zachary was on his way. At that point, I was starting to really miss my family. I would see my aunt and my abuelita once in a while. But I wanted to change my life so that I could make them proud and start having them more present in my life. My family was really good people; they love me and just wanted the best for me and my children.

I also began to notice that my husband struggled with addiction, not to drugs; he was addicted to stealing. He was the definition of a kleptomaniac. For anyone reading this, I hope that it is easy for you to recognize all the things that I overlooked or chose to ignore, and how they affected my life along the way. This was just one more of those things. It wasn't his fault; it was the environment that we lived in.

At this point, I decided I didn't want to live in a trailer park anymore. I wanted better things for my family, and I wanted to get an education for myself. So, I enrolled in a community college, and told my husband that we needed to move.

There were some arguments about moving out of the trailer park. I had expected there to be since that's what he'd known his whole life. His parents lived there, his brother lived next door to us, and all of his friends lived there as well. Moving out of the trailer park was not something he was going to plan for himself. If I wanted this change for our family, I was going to have to do the work.

There was a day when I finally went to find a house. It was in a very nice neighborhood. I went home and told him I'd be signing the lease and letting the trailer park people repossess our trailer home. I didn't care about my credit or realized this choice might damage it for the future. In my mind, I wanted my children to grow up in a much better environment; and thought that if I got him away from that area, maybe there would be less stealing.

Right before we moved, on June 23, 2004, we brought our beautiful baby boy into the world. He had the brightest blue eyes and the finest blond hair. He changed my world forever. My life, as I had pictured it from as far back as I could remember, was completely everything I wanted it to be. I had a husband, two beautiful babies that I always prayed for, and we were moving into a beautiful four-bedroom home.

We fixed up our new house really nice, and everything seemed perfect. At the beginning of our marriage, I worried about being able to provide, but that was no longer an issue at this time of our lives. My husband was working construction, and I was working in sales. We were making really good money between the two of us.

Every night, we would come home, cook dinner together, bathe the kids after dinner, put them to bed, and have "Mommy and Daddy" time. We always made sure to have this time to ourselves each evening. Our typical day-to-day looked pretty much the same routine. My kids had the type of household that I never really knew as a kid. No chaotic childhood or partying teens supervising- just Mom and Dad every day while living in a nice neighborhood.

Since I worked in retail sales, there were some evenings and most weekends where I had to work. On those days, my husband would often show up at the mall with the kids and surprise me. I always loved seeing the three of them.

At this point, my uncle was now starting to talk to me, and my aunt and Abuelita would often offer to watch the kids. My husband never really allowed that, however, because he always said they were our kids, and no one should watch them but us. He'd rarely let his parents keep them overnight, but would once in a while. I always just found him to be a super protective, loving, father. I especially thought him and Kait had a super close bond. They were attached to each other's hip. Wherever he went, Kait followed.

One beautiful sunny day, Kait was playing in her kiddy pool while I sat next to it with Zach in my lap. Kait was two and Zach was barely a couple of months old. Daddy came home from work and walked into the backyard with a surprise. It was the most beautiful little hound dog with tiny little legs and huge floppy ears. His eyes were the definition of puppy-dog eyes. Kait was ecstatic, and I, of course, melted at the gesture. We quickly fell in love with this puppy.

But a couple days later, there was a startling knock at our door. The kids and I were home alone. When I opened the door, there were a ton of cops at our door, and confusion set it. I didn't understand what was happening. The cops were screaming, asking for my husband, with their guns drawn. My heart was beating so hard. I could feel the vibration in my eardrums and felt dizzy, as if on the verge of losing consciousness from the confusion. All I could hear was my kids crying in the background. My little Kait stood in front of the door, watching the cops hollering their demands. Tears rolled down her cheeks. All I wanted to do was comfort her as some of them rushed into the house, while others continued questioning the whereabouts of my husband.

Some of the officers came back to the door with our new puppy. Apparently, that little hound dog was the reason for the whole situation. It turned out that my husband had decided to steal the pup from one of the homes that his construction company had been working on. I guess since the site was an hour away, he didn't think anyone would suspect him for the theft. He never made it home from work that day.

Instead, for the first time in my life, I had to figure out how to bail someone out of jail. It took a few days, not to mention, he was already on probation from when he was released from prison the first time, so this was a violation of his probation. He was looking at possibly going back to prison. Still, to this day, I can remember the uneasiness and terrified feeling I felt in my chest.

The man I loved was looking at prison time, and never in a billion years had I pictured myself being a single mother.

He convinced me that I needed to speak to the woman who had filed the charges against him. He knew where she lived, so he gave me the address to get in touch with her. I was desperate to keep my husband out of prison, so I drove to her house, and also attempted to call her a few times. When she finally agreed to meet with me, the wavy black-haired thin woman approached me with a feisty demeanor. She had a heavy accent, you could tell that she wasn't comfortable speaking English, so to make her more comfortable I switched to Spanish. Her frustration lessened a bit, and she explained to me that she bred these puppies regularly for the sheriff's department. It made sense now why the officers were so aggressive during our encounter over a puppy. I was extremely apologetic to her. I explained that I understood what he had done was beyond wrong, but that he was only thinking about surprising his family, and not weighing out the consequences. I described to her the man I knew, and I begged her to please drop the charges as I just could not bear the thought of being a single mother, and we both knew that this would mean prison for him as they charged him with grand theft. We spoke a few times after that, and I can't remember if it was before the court date or at the court, but she finally decided to drop the charges. She clearly told me that she didn't do it for him, she did it for me and the kids.

He was free to continue being the loving husband and father I knew him to be. This little mishap could now be put behind us, and our fairy-tale life could continue on as it should. Only, because of the choices he'd made, life couldn't simply pick back up as usual. He lost his job, and since daycare was super expensive, he became a stay-at-home dad. I was working a lot of hours to sustain the household bills, but I felt comforted, knowing that he was home with the kids. They could keep him grounded, and he would keep them safe.

Chapter 7

A Monster in the Closet

One day, my husband frantically called me at work to tell me that our 6-month-old baby boy had fallen off the bed. He needed me to get home right away because Zach wouldn't stop crying, and he didn't know what was wrong. I left work. The usual 30-minute drive down Highway 27 felt like it had turned into a four-hour detour. When I walked into the house, everything was eerily quiet. I had suspected Zach to still be screaming, and immediately asked where he was. He told me Zach had finally went to sleep, and I should leave him alone.

Obviously, "leaving him alone" is the last thing a mother does when she's just spent what felt like four hours worrying about the health of her son. I went into Zachary's room and found him lying in his bed asleep. I felt so relieved to see him. I noticed a bruise on his face and pick him up to get a closer look. The second I touched his leg; I heard the most horrific scream I have ever heard come out of a baby. It reminded me of a hurt dog yipping for help.

I rushed out of the room, and told my husband I was taking Zachary to the hospital. As I was getting his diaper bag and buckling him into his car seat, I asked my husband where the bruise on Zach's face came from. He replied that he must have got it in the fall. The vacuum cleaner was next to the bed when Zach rolled off the side of it, so he must have hit his face on the vacuum during the fall. He told me that he would have his parents watch Kait while we took Zach to the hospital.

But when they arrived, he decided that he would stay to watch Kait with his dad while his mother and I drove Zachary to the hospital. After some x-rays, it was determined that Zachary had a hairline fracture on his femur. As we waited for the doctors in the room, two ladies walked into the room. One of the ladies was wearing a black leather jacket. She had curly blonde chin-length hair, and looked to be around the mid-40s. The other was a uniformed police officer with a long black ponytail and a huge camera hanging from her neck. The lady with the leather jacket introduced herself, with a smoker's voice, as a detective. She informed me and my mother-in-law it was protocol for them to ask me questions, and wanted to know in detail what happened to my son. I began telling her about Zach falling off the bed and she kept asking where I was when it happened. I was still wearing my blue Nextel button-up shirt and black slacks from work. I explained that I was at work, as my clothes clearly suggested, and would only be able to tell her what my husband had told me. While this was going on, the lady in the police uniform was taking pictures of my son. By the end of the conversation, or interrogation, as that is what it felt like, it was around 4 AM. They asked if they could follow me to my house to speak to my husband and two-year-old daughter.

My mother-in-law could not believe that they wanted to question her son. She was insistent that he could never do anything to hurt Zachary. I called my husband on our way to the house from the hospital. A bit surprised that he hadn't called to check on us, I told him there was a detective wanting to speak to him about what happened to Zachary. At first, he replied, "Oh shit. Oh shit. Why do they want to talk to me?" Then he changed his tone and calmly replied, "Of course, whatever they need."

When I walked into the house, I had to do a double-take- it was spotless! Not a single toy on the floor. Even on a good day, with a toddler and a baby, there were a few toys that got left around. But the house had been cleaned as if we were about to entertain company.

As soon as the detective entered our home, she began questioning my husband. The officer with the ponytail asked me to wake Kait up and undress her so that she could inspect her body for bruises. Zachary was back asleep, so I laid him on his bed and took the officer to Kait's room.

The detective ended the questioning by asking my husband if he would voluntarily leave the house and stay with his parents for the night. She told us that he would still be able to see me and the kids, but not before I took Zachary for some forensic testing first thing in the morning. Which, since it was already early morning, would only be a few more hours away.

The forensic testing facility was located in a town called Bartow. It was an hour-long drive for me, Kait, and Zach. I wasn't sure what to expect when we arrived. The raspy-voiced detective and ponytailed officer met me there. They put my six-month-old under an ultra violet machine. Shortly after, the detective came out and told me that the bruise on my son was indicative of a hand print across my son's face. Needless to say, but I'll say it anyway, I was in shock and refused to believe her. There was no way that my husband was capable of what she had suggested. There was no way he would do such a thing to his son.

She knew that I was in denial, and patiently explained that my husband had done this to my child. She began explaining to me with many hand gestures how baby's little bones are more like rubber at that age. A hairline fracture, like Zachary's, could only be caused by twisting the baby's leg with extreme physical force. Falling off a bed, in her professional opinion, could in no way create the kind of injury Zach had received.

I left the facility in disbelief. I called my husband and immediately began letting him know what they were saying. In his deep and calm demeanor, he told me that they were only saying this because they were prejudging him due to his prior criminal background. He assured me over and over that he never would harm our child. As he spoke, I felt super guilty for believing the detective's accusations could even be plausible. By the time I made the hour drive home, he was waiting at the house for the kids and me. I sighed with relief, fully convinced of his innocence. We would just put this behind us.

42

The kids went down for a nap, and my cell phone rang. It was the scratchy-voiced detective on the other line. She asked me if I had seen my husband. She had gone to his parents' house to talk with him, but he was not there. I, of course, told her that he was sitting next to me on our back patio. She told me to please wait there for her as she had a few questions for us, and was stopping by. When I hung up and told my husband what the detective had said, he told me he was going to hop in the shower real quick.

I remember thinking that was a weird choice and saying, "A shower now? She's on her way."

But he proceeded to the walk-in shower in the master bathroom. Within minutes, there was a knock on the front door. It was the detective, accompanied by four uniformed officers. This feisty detective was no more than 5'6," yet she asked me, "Where is he?" in a very commanding tone.

I responded, "He hopped in the shower real quick."

The four officers rushed into the house and proceeded to the bedroom. They pulled his butt-naked body straight out of the shower. The detective slammed his 6'5" tall body down to the ground, handcuffing him, as she read him his Miranda rights. She said he was being charged with aggravated child abuse. The officers assisted him with putting on some clothes before they took him from the house.

The same fear that had rushed over me the first time he had been arrested rushed over me once more. As they rushed him out to the squad car in handcuffs, I was trying to plead with the detective, walking behind them towards the car, and she kept telling me to go back inside; I was extremely upset, and as they shoved him in the back seat, I yelled at the detective, telling her that she was making a huge mistake. There was no way that he would do anything to harm our child. After our earlier phone call, he had me convinced that was the truth. I had never known him to be violent, so why wouldn't it be.

He was so amazing and overprotective with our daughter, especially because she was "Daddy's little girl." He couldn't, he wouldn't do anything to hurt our baby boy. I was planning to stand by him through it all. They had obviously gotten their facts terribly wrong.

Never could I imagine what the next few years of our lives would bring.

Chapter 8

The Beginning of an Awakening

The court battle was long and lengthy, and it ended quite unexpectedly with my husband taking a plea bargain. He pled "guilty" to a lesser charge of child abuse. His attorney and I were shocked that he decided to take a plea when he was "innocent." He convinced me that it was all for me and the kids. He wanted to avoid going to trial and didn't want to risk being taken away from his family.

A few years passed. Life was back to normal...well, normal for us.

My husband couldn't find a job because of his extensive criminal rap sheet. And even when he did have a job, he couldn't keep it for one reason or another. This left me always having to sustain the household. I was always working and got to be home with the kids. The whole situation resulted in us constantly arguing, which was beginning to put a strain on our marriage.

Throughout the entire process, his addiction hadn't gone away. One day, he took the kids to JCPenney, put new shoes on our son, and walked out of the store. Another time, he attempted to steal a watch from Target, and was caught red-handed by their security. There were even times when we'd go shopping together, and he'd ask me to put things in the diaper bag. As if his problem wasn't enough, he was now wrapping me and the kids into it. It got to the point where going shopping was extremely stressful, and I just didn't want any part of it.

We didn't need to steal!

Even though I was the only one working, I made decent money. So, it wasn't a survival thing, it was just an addiction that I couldn't help him overcome. An addiction that he obviously had no desire to admit to or get rid of. Eventually, the arguments began to escalate. By this time, the kids were four and six.

The attentive husband I once had was disappearing; it's as if he didn't want to be around me, but would get upset if I went anywhere with my family or friends. His demeanor began to change towards me for the first time ever. I figured everything would pass and we'd work everything out. After all, when I married him, I thought we'd be together forever.

Looking back on all this, the worst part was not realizing what the children had to endure while I was working. Both kids would cry at the door every time I left for work, especially Zachary, but I always thought it was because they wanted Mom. That's a normal thing for kids, right? I never thought there could ever be underlying issues.

A few months passed – things seemed to be quieting down, and then I got another phone call.

He had been arrested for shoplifting once again. I was so fed up with everything that I told him, "This is the last time I will ever bail you out."

I'm not sure how he took those words, but from that point forward, he started consuming himself in a virtual world called *World of Warcraft*. He'd stay up all night and sleep all day. It was as if the real world no longer existed. The house was a mess, the kids were a mess. And one day, I had enough. I stood by his computer, begging for his attention, begging for him to talk to me. Furious that my pleas weren't enough to get his attention, I marched into our garage. If he was so consumed by the game that he wouldn't acknowledge my existence, it was time for me to take drastic measures. So, I did what any scorned woman might do- I flipped off the circuit breakers!

When I walked back into the house, he was furious that I had turned off his game. He forced me back into the garage and locked the door. I couldn't see to turn the breakers back on or unlock the door. All I could do was stand in the dark, banging on the door, begging for him to let me back in. I could hear Kait crying on the other side of the door, asking him to let me back in. He told her to go back to bed, and left me locked out in the garage for hours. We didn't talk for days.

That weekend was Kait's birthday party. We were having a ton of friends and family over around noon. It was around 10 in the morning. A beautiful sunny Florida day, I was playing music pretty loud, trying to get him motivated and out of bed. I asked him several times to get out of bed so we could go to the store and pick up last-minute things. It was his daughter's birthday, there was no reason for him to sleep the day away and miss her party. Once again, he had been up all night playing his game, so the only thing I'd get in reply was, "I'm tired, let me sleep. Turn off the music."

I insisted over and over. He finally got up, came out in the living room, and yelled "I said turn the fucking music down, I'm trying to sleep." He walked up to the stereo and turned it down.

As he was walking back to our bedroom, I turned it back up. Suddenly, the next thing I know, my face whipped to one side, leaving a sting. He had slapped me and told me to turn the music off! That was the first time he ever hit me, and the first time I knew that he had also hit our baby boy. For years I struggled with the what if. What if he had hit Zachary that day? What if the detective was right? But I would tell myself that I was crazy, he'd never harm me or the kids.

His parents arrived early. I was crying and told them I didn't know what was going on with him. He wouldn't come out of the bedroom. His mom and dad both tried talking to him and convincing him to leave the bedroom, but he told them to leave him the fuck alone and stayed in bed. I was pretty close with his mother, and she apologized for his behavior. Then she asked if we had gotten in a fight. I told her what had happened, and she said I probably should have left him alone. Yes, she pretty much said it was my own fault that he had slapped me. I never realized

48

it at the time, but she always had a way of manipulating things when it came to her son. She never wanted to believe he did anything wrong.

He stayed in the bedroom for the entire birthday party. After everyone left that night, he got out of bed and went straight to his computer. I walked up to him, wanting to talk. I wanted to know why he would punish our daughter and miss her birthday. Much to my surprise, it immediately escalated. He put me in a choke hold. I started crying and frantically screaming. I repeatedly asked, "How could you?"

How could he punish Kait? Why had he slapped me? Why was he choking me? What on earth had gotten into him? But instead of getting a response, I was drug across the house by my hair. He kicked me and choked me. I must have lost consciousness at some point because I remember waking up to him pouring ice water on me. He was kicking me, saying, "Get the fuck up, you're not going to die on me. Get up."

Everything around me was blurry and unrecognizable. I was terrified. All I could think about was needing to get out of the house. I managed to get up and run out of the house. I ran across the street to our neighbor's house. The neighbors pointed out that I was soaked. I assumed it was from the iced water, but I will never forget the neighbor said, "Honey, you peed." All I could think about as I stood there with the neighbors were the kids. Despite what had just transpired, I was afraid of calling the cops at that moment. It was a fear that he had instilled in me throughout our eight years together. According to his logic, cops were never helpful in any situation.

The neighbors decided to walk across the street and talk to him. He assured them the kids were fine and somehow convinced them I was the neurotic one. They told me that the kids would be fine for the night, and they would walk over with me in the morning to pick them up.

Chapter 9

A Fresh Start

At that point, I realized that I absolutely must get my children out of the house and away from him. The neighbors helped me pick up the kids the next morning. I loaded them in the car and drove away. I'm not sure that I really had a plan beyond that. Some kind of survival mode had been switched on inside me, and the safety of my children was the only thing that mattered. I was too embarrassed to go to my family. After all, they had warned me before I even married him not to get involved with him. I went to the only friend that I had left. It was her birthday and she was having friends and family over for a party.

I told her I didn't feel good and she let me lay in her bed. While I was lying down, I started hyperventilating. My face went numb and my lips began to tingle. I didn't know what was happening to me and thought I was going to pass out. My friend, who was periodically checking on me, told me that I didn't look very well. I told her I thought I was dying. She told her husband to watch my kids, and left her party to take me to the hospital.

The doctor noticed I had bruises around my neck. My friend told the doctor everything that had happened. Before I knew it, detectives were in my hospital room, asking me where my husband was. While they were there, he called to check on me. He wanted to reassure me that we could work everything out if I came back home. The detectives asked me to keep him on the line and feed me things to tell him. They sent officers to the house to arrest him while I was on the phone with him. He was arrested for domestic violence and would be looking at 5 to 10 years in prison. All the courts needed was for me to testify. They referred me to a domestic violence unit in Polk County. This unit helped me move with the kids and file for a restraining order against my husband. They also set me up with an attorney to help me file for divorce. Since everything was so backed up with the courts, the date was set for a year out.

I believe he spent a total of ten months in jail. In my mind, it was over. The court date for our divorce was set. The logical side of me said, "Never again." But my heart had a completely different opinion. My heart wanted to hold on to the tiny shred of hope. Somewhere along the way, I met a really nice guy, and for a few months, my mind won. I began dating him. I was determined to move on and find a different life. Unfortunately, I was under the awful illusion that you had to get under someone to get over someone. I really should have taken some time to figure out who I was without my now soon-to-be husband, but the thought never crossed my mind back then.

For whatever reason, I never testified against him. I suppose if I had to name a reason it would be that he was my children's father and I felt terrible that he could spend time in prison. I knew what him going to prison the first time had done to his mother, and I just didn't want her or my children to go through that. His attorney ended up having the state drop the charges, because without my testimony, they had nothing to convict him. There was an order of protection in place for me and the kids, but that didn't matter. Once he was released, he got to me. He fed me his lies that things would be different and my fairy-tale hungry heart went back to him.

I broke it off with the nice guy in hopes that things had changed. This would be our happily-ever-after moment. I warned my husband, if for any reason, he ended up back in jail, that would be the end of us. I kept our date in court for the divorce. He wasn't very happy about it, but I told him we could go through with it and once we worked things out get remarried. As you can probably imagine, or maybe you're hoping, it ended a few months later. He was pulled over on the way to work for driving with a suspended license. I got the call in the middle of the night that I needed to come bail him out. I refused, and that was the end of us.

Once again, my mind and heart were battling each other. My mind was wise enough to accept that it was time to finalize our divorce. It was also time to move away, far enough away to where it would no longer be easy to return to him. I had to get my kids away from this toxic environment. The instability, the fighting, the violence, Daddy in and out of jail-none of that was right. So, I decided to go to court and finalize our divorce.

Unfortunately, my heart was sick and delusional. It tried convincing me that moving would be the best choice because he would follow us and we could fix our family. If he could just get away from all that he knew, far enough away that he, too, couldn't easily return, we could start fresh, and he'd be a changed man.

He begged me not to finalize the divorce. He was so against it that he didn't even show up to court.

I will never forget the judge, an older man with a black balding hairline, asking me where my soon-to-be ex-husband was. I told him that he refused to show up. The judge went over my husband's criminal record and then asked me, "What type of custody agreement do you want to have with him? What type of visitation schedule do you find reasonable?"

Although my attorney was sitting right next to me, I responded to him by saying "Your Honor, I realize what his record says, but he is a good father, so he should get normal visitation."

The judge stared back at me. "Ma'am with all due respect, he beat you and was convicted of child abuse for breaking your son's leg. This man will NOT have unsupervised visitation with your children until they're sixteen years of age and old enough to protect themselves."

Having the judge override my decision came as a shock. I imagine it was probably more so about having to break the news to my *now* ex-husband. But when I look back now, I am so grateful and relieved for that wonderful man. The judge saw something in those criminal records that I had been blinded to.

I left the courthouse crying. I'm not sure if it was the realization that my marriage was finally over or the realization that he'd be pissed when he heard the custody arrangement. For whatever reason, he was the first person that I called. When I told him the judge's ruling regarding the kids, he began crying, "How could you do this?"

Me? He was going to blame me for this? I knew then that I had to make a drastic change for my babies. A couple of weeks later, I packed a U-Haul and decided to leave Florida forever. The worst part was having to break the news to everyone.

For years, my family and friends noticed how controlling he was and warned me to divorce him. Instead of listening to their advice, I slowly cut them off one by one until it was too late. I had no one else in Florida. I damaged a lot of relationships for him because he and the kids were my world! The family I always wanted. My own!

My family and friends kept asking me to stay, but I knew if I stayed, I would just keep going back to him, and nothing would change. I was truly in love, and leaving him was the absolute hardest decision I ever had to make- I didn't see the bad in the midst of it. I was blinded by love. The last thing in the world that I ever wanted was a broken home for my children. In my mind, I always thought, "He'll get better, he'll change." He had his issues, but he was like a drug to me. I couldn't think straight when

I was around him. I even told him the day of our divorce we could get remarried once we work on our issues. Together we could get away from Florida and get a fresh start. All I could ever think about was how I could make it work with him. And for that reason alone, I had to leave.

His mother begged me not to take the kids. I felt terrible, but I knew I had to do it. Zachary was six, Kait was eight...we said our goodbyes to their grandparents in a grocery store parking lot. Then, with a U-Haul trailer attached to my Dodge Durango, off we went into the night. I drove most of the night while the kids slept. I listened to music to stay distracted and focused on what my mind was telling me to do and not my heart.

Initially, I intended to move to Georgia, where I had applied for a job at Delta. However, the thought of being all alone in Georgia felt a bit overwhelming. Living as a single mom, all alone, had never been part of my plan. I skipped Georgia, and decided to move to Illinois because I had an aunt and two cousins there. That way, if there was an emergency, I'd at least be able to call on them.

The life I had known for the past eight years was now in my rearview mirror. I was in a completely unfamiliar place. And I was scared of the unknown.

Even as I took these steps to walk away, I secretly hoped he would follow his family, and we could once again work on that fairy-tale ending. Thankfully, he was on probation, so he couldn't move out of state any time soon.

The kids and I moved into a two-bedroom townhouse in a cute little town called Sycamore. It was the kind of town you might see in a Hallmark movie; small town in the middle of nowhere with plenty of historical buildings. At the time, I had an interpretation job from home. It was kind of perfect. I didn't need to have a sitter because the kids would come home from school, and I would be waiting for them. Adapting to our new life was pretty easy.

I also didn't waste any time getting into the dating scene. Again, I found myself thinking that having a guy in my life was the best plan. Then three months after my divorce, I found out I was pregnant. I was terrified. I never wanted to be a single parent, especially not of three kids. Then there was the awful feeling that I had committed adultery. Yes, I know, our divorce was final and I was dating other men. But deep down, I had hoped my ex-husband would follow us up North, and we would fix our little family.

For whatever reason, he was the first person I called. I cried as I told him the reason for my call, "I want you to hear it from me and not from someone else that I'm pregnant."

He was livid, yet his response was baffling, he told me, "If the baby is a girl, I will consider raising her with you. But if you're pregnant with another man's son, never. That will be the end of us."

For a brief moment, that little ray of hope was still on the horizon. If the baby was a girl, then we might still have a chance to fix our family. That hope was extinguished two weeks later, however, when his mother called me to tell me he had gotten married to his high school sweetheart. Wow, not even two weeks earlier, he was talking about helping me raise a baby, and now he was remarried. Guess it didn't take him long to move on either.

It was time that I shut that door and really start focusing on this new life. The kids were adjusting nicely. Maybe moving on entirely was exactly what I needed to do as well. When I was two months pregnant, the baby's father and I decided to move in together. We wanted to see if we could build a life together. Well…if I am being honest, it wasn't really a mutual decision. One day, he came over to our townhouse, and never left. Everything was happening super fast! The tiny two-bedroom town house was quickly feeling crowded, but everything seemed to be working out okay.

When I hit about four months pregnant, there was a terrible blizzard outside. It was a super cold February afternoon. The kids and I, being from Florida, were fascinated by the snow. We'd never experiencing anything like a blizzard before, so we decided to bundle up and go outside. There was a giant mound of snow in our front yard. We decided that would be the best place to start our snow adventure. Zachary was wearing a black skeleton hoodie that zipped up over his head, and Kait was wearing a pink scarf and Cookie Monster beanie; the two of them just laughing and playing in the snow so joyfully. For the first time in a long time, I felt extreme contentment. Things were great. The fear of the unknown was quickly vanishing.

Chapter 10

Unveiling the Truth

Moving my children across the country, away from everyone they knew, was something that weighed heavy on me. Thankfully, Kait and Zachary were always super close. So, while they left cousins and friends, each of them still had their best friend to hang out with. They had an incredible bond.

One of my fondest memories was when Zachary was in kindergarten. It was his very first book fair at school. I had given him money to buy books with his class, and when I picked him up from school that afternoon, his teacher, giggling, told me, "I tried to get him to buy a book that was more for a boy, but he refused."

When Zach got in the car, I asked him to show me what he bought at the book fair, and he pulled out a Hannah Montana book. He had the biggest smile as he said, "I bought it for my big sister."

He melted my heart. That's the kind of love he always had for his big sister.

Aside from leaving behind friends and family, another fear that crossed my mind after we moved was their father. How would the kids feel being so far away from their dad? I continued to stay in touch with him through phone calls for the first three months of our divorce. But once he got remarried, he cut off all communication with us.

To my surprise, they didn't really say much about their dad not being around. Zachary had always been closer to me, so I supposed that I shouldn't have been surprised by that, but Kait had always been Daddy's little girl. He never let her leave his side, and they seemed to have a special bond.

She never asked about her dad, but I could tell that his absence had to be bothering her. Something was bothering her. She seemed very standoffish, and there was a total change in her demeanor. I knew she couldn't bottle it up, so I would often try to get her to open up. I wanted to know how she was feeling, what she was thinking in that little eight-year-old mind of hers. And deep down, wanted to know she didn't hate me for moving her away from her father. But she wouldn't say a word.

Then one day, when I was around six months pregnant, our little life got flipped around once more.

Kait and Zach were upstairs playing in their room as usual. I was downstairs cleaning the kitchen. The house was peaceful; a little too peaceful with two children. That awful mom feeling set into my stomach. It was WAY too quiet for them, which usually meant they were being kids, up to no good- coloring on walls, sneaking fruit snacks, or something.

I walked upstairs. I expected empty wrappers or crayons dumped on the floor, but what I saw shocked and horrified me. They were playing inappropriately, doing things kids should not be doing or even know how to do. I quickly grabbed them both by the hand and asked them what they were doing and where they learned to do that.

"Kait showed me," Zach quickly ratted her out. I'm sure he could tell by my actions and tone that they had obviously done something wrong. But I'm also sure that he wasn't quite sure why it was wrong.

I took Kait downstairs to the living room couch and asked her where she learned to do it. She put her little head down and would not say anything except, "I don't know."

Although I was doing my best to stay calm so I wouldn't scare her, I was absolutely freaking out inside, wondering where my child had been exposed to such things. I kept trying to get her to talk to me and tell me where she learned what she had taught her brother. I explained I just wanted to know where she had learned those things. I certainly didn't watch pornography, nor had I ever done anything where they could accidentally have seen any kind of "meant for the bedroom" type act.

Since I was unable to get answers on my own, I decided to contact my employee helpline. I talked to a counselor over the phone. The counselor told me that family counseling was covered through my employee plan. She set up counseling appointments with a specialist at a child counseling center. The employee plan allowed for each of us to visit with our own counselor. God knows I needed it just as much as they did! Six months pregnant, and you discover your kids doing things they should not know how to do. I was an emotional wreck! But I knew that seeing the counselors would be the best option for all of us. If Kait wouldn't tell me, hopefully she would talk with the counselor.

I pulled up to a brown building. As we walked across the parking lot, I reassured the kids that this was a safe place for them to talk about anything. They could tell the counselor about anything they were feeling. I would never be mad at them about anything that they said. I just wanted to know where they had learned to do what they had done.

On our first visit, I felt some separation anxiety as each kid went into their own room with their own counselor. When it was my turn to meet my counselor, she didn't even get her name out before I was hysterically crying. It was as if she'd popped the cork on the champagne bottle of my life. The last eight years of my life spewed from my mouth. The guilt of walking away from my marriage poured out first. Was that possibly the reason my kids were acting out? Were they upset with me for leaving their father? Or maybe it was because I was now pregnant with another man's child. I was sure that I was the one to blame someway somehow. I just wanted to know how in the world I could have missed my children being exposed to something so awful.

To my surprise, the counselor bypassed all the blame I had put on myself and asked if I had ever thought of the possibility that maybe the children had been sexually abused. I felt absolutely nauseous at the thought. She explained that kids who were sexually abused typically act out or role play on other kids. I kept thinking of a million things throughout the years that could have possibly been signs, but I just didn't even want to think that it could be a possibility.

I cried for days after the counseling session. Kait would come into my room at night. She'd lay in bed with me, and I could see she was concerned over my emotion. I would tell her, "Honey, if anyone has ever touched your privates, I don't care who it is, I just need to know. I'm always going to love you no matter what."

I always felt as if she wanted to tell me something, but she would not. She would just say, "I love you, goodnight." And go to her bed.

At that point, I had separated the kids. I didn't allow them to sleep in the same room anymore. Deep down, I was mortified to think that something could happen again. Zach was sleeping on the couch, and we were looking for bigger places so they could each have their own bedroom.

We continued going to counseling once a week, and suddenly, Kait's counselor told me that Kait had drawn a picture for her. She needed to sit with me and discuss what Kait had drawn. The picture was of what appeared to be butt cheeks drawn in red ink. The word "red" was written about ten times all over each cheek. The counselor told me that when she asked Kait what the red was, she had replied, "Pain." It stung.

At that point, the counselor made a report to the state's Department of Children and Family Services. An investigation was started. Days that felt more like weeks passed by. Kait still would not say anything to me. I'm sure she must have tired of me asking her, pleading with her to tell me something, but she refused to talk.

Then, one day, she came to me and asked, "Mommy, are we ever going to see my daddy again?"

I wasn't quite sure how to answer her question. It had been about three months since we had heard from him. I really wasn't sure if they ever would see their dad again. I didn't want to shatter her hopes, so I decided to respond with a neutral answer, "Well, honey, I'm not sure. Why, do you want to see him?"

To my surprise, she quickly shook her head no.

My heart raced and my body felt hot all over. I was nervous to ask why Daddy's little girl, the one who had such a special bond, had no desire to see him. "Oh, you don't? How come, sweetie? We don't have to see him ever again if you don't want to."

Right at that moment, my worst fears became a reality as she cried, "He used to touch my privates."

Chapter 11

Time to Be Honest...with Myself

How could the man that I loved, the one I had married, do this to our own child? I felt disgusted, angry, and confused. I didn't understand. Was this the reason why he could raise another man's daughter, but not a son? I didn't want to believe what I was hearing, but this time, I could not make the same mistake as before. This time I was HEARING it from my own child, straight from her mouth, so I had to believe her no matter what. I had to protect her no matter what.

I felt horrible as her mother, knowing that her innocence had been stripped from her and the relationship that she had with her father all along, the "special bond" that I thought existed between the two of them was anything but appropriate. He was supposed to be the one person on the planet to help me protect my children, not harm them. I was shattered.

I promised her that she would ***never*** have to see him again. She began to tell me that her dad had always told her that if she ever said anything to anyone, I would hate her, and the cops would take her away. What he did with her was their secret, and she wasn't allowed to tell anyone. I let her know that she never had to be scared to tell me anything.

67

The Department of Children and Family Services (DCFS) in Illinois deemed my home to be safe. However, because the abuse took place in Florida, there was nothing they could do except refer us to the DCFS office in Florida. Unfortunately, DCFS in Florida would not take the case since the kids now lived in Illinois. It seemed like everyone wanted to help, but kept getting stopped by red-tape laws or state line limitations. The entire thing was an awful legal mess. The Sycamore Police Department put us in touch with the Haines City Police Department in Florida, in the city where we had lived at the time the abuse took place.

Every single night for months throughout the remainder of my pregnancy was torturous. Not only was I exhausted from seeking justice for my little girl, but because Kait finally felt safe, she let me hear every detail. Not just a few. I'm talking about every single detail from as far back as she could remember. A lot of the times, it wasn't even what she said but instead what she drew or re-enacted with her stuffed animals. She'd bring me all kinds of disturbing drawings or re-enacted things that happened. Things that no child would even know about unless they had lived through it. I would stay strong for her, but end up crying myself to sleep. I couldn't believe that my little girl had endured so much in her eight years of life. Or worse, that I had been blind to everything that was happening. Lincoln's father worked the graveyard shift, so me and the kids were always home by ourselves in the evenings. I am grateful that on many sleepless nights, I could at least call him and get the horrifying stories off my chest.

Amongst all the turmoil, on August 3rd, 2011, I gave birth to a beautiful healthy baby boy, Lincoln. We moved into a new house to accommodate our growing family. Through all of this, Lincoln's father and I were still attempting to create a family.

During Kait's investigation, the police took my ex-husband in for questioning. While he was talking with the detective, he had the nerve to say that I was a bitter scorned ex-wife and was making it all up. Why on earth would I ever make up such horrendous stories regarding my little girl? The crazy part was that the detective who took the case on ended up being one of the officers who was there the day he was arrested for abusing me. He knew exactly what kind of man he was and did everything he could to fight for our family. Eventually, despite everything that we had gone through, the entire investigation came down to Kait. The police wanted her to testify in court against her father.

She was ten years old now, but he had obviously ingrained the same distrust towards public authorities that he had initially instilled in me. I'm not sure if she still thought the police might take her away or if it was the fear of confronting him, but Kait did not want to testify. I had promised her that she would never have to see him again, so there was no way that I was going to break that promise in the name of justice. With that being said, the investigation was closed as "not enough evidence for a conviction." The detective called me and told me how sorry he was that he wasn't able to do anything more for the case.

After the investigation was closed, I began taking a hard look at our lives. So much had happened over the past ten years. The counseling sessions helped me process through everything that had taken place. There was all the guilt, animosity, and pain that I harbored towards my ex-husband. I had been so blinded by love that there was so much I had failed to see. I'd somehow lost sight of my own worth along the way, and on top of that, failed to protect my children.

I had to take a hard look at my relationship with Lincoln's father. Unfortunately, the relationship never really had a chance. It was toxic from the start, and finding all this out about my daughter put a huge strain on me emotionally to even attempt to make a relationship work. I finally had to admit to myself that there was no future for the two of us. I had jumped from one bad relationship into another. I just could not see myself trying to make it work anymore, and it eventually led us into a courtroom where I found myself fighting for custody of my Lincoln. It was a lengthy and costly custody battle, but in 2014, it was finalized. I walked out of that courtroom with my head held high. I had taken a stand for my child; things were going to be different from this moment on.

Through many talks, and even more tears, me and the kids were finally in a place where we could move forward with our lives. As I examined the things we had gone through, I had to acknowledge there were events that happened along the way, that even though I thought were bad at the time, I recognized they were actually God graciously protecting us along the way.

One of those was the judge in the divorce court that wouldn't allow me to let my ex have unsupervised visitations. Then there was getting pregnant with Lincoln. That wasn't at all a part of my plan but Lincoln had certainly been Kait's guardian angel on earth. Getting pregnant with him pushed my ex out of the picture. Up to that point, I had thought about us getting back together, but that door closed when I got pregnant with a son, and he got remarried. With that door closed, I believe it opened the door for Kait to finally feel safe enough to tell me everything.

From that day forward, I promised myself and my children that for them, I would build my strength and give them the best life I possibly could.

Chapter 12

A New Chapter of Life

This is the part where I pause for a moment and simply take a breath. I'm not sure if it has been as nerve-racking to read this as it was to live through and then relive through every detail once more while writing this book, but I just need to take a brief moment.

I began the book with the Forrest Gump quote, "Life was like a box of chocolates, you never know what you're gonna get." And I truly stand by that. I was hoping for that chocolate-covered cherry kind of love and marriage, but ended up disappointed with the coconut-filled divorce. At some point, I even felt like someone set my box of chocolates in the hot Florida sunshine, letting them all melt together until nothing was recognizable.

Ten years seems like an eternity when you're younger, but once you're older, it's much more like a quick blink of the eye. The past ten years had been filled with so many crazy details. Some of them brought on by my own choices, and some of them thrown out of nowhere from the choices of others. So much stuff to process through, and yet, the story isn't over yet.

As the years went on, I built myself up into a good career. I was making the most money I had ever made in my life. This allowed me to enroll Zachary and Kait into a private middle school. Although Zachary and Kait had been through a lot, they were really excelling. Life seemed pretty calm, and dare I say, normal. For Kait's birthday one year, I even surprised her with a "real life unicorn" – a beautiful black horse. Since I could remember, every birthday when I would ask her what she wanted, she'd say "a unicorn." So one day, I decided I was going to get a horse, and I spent hours making a unicorn headband with sparkles and all to surprise her. I found a boarding facility for our horse, and we'd go together as a family to learn everything we could about horses. Kait got into volleyball and seemed to transform from an anti-social child into a social butterfly.

Zachary had become a pretty popular kid in school and was always trying new things. He tried wrestling, baseball, volleyball, he was even in a school play. He never seemed to be able to stick to sports; however, music, reading, and participating in school plays really kept him occupied. I also enrolled him in the Big Brothers Big Sisters of America club, and he had been matched up with a "Big Brother" who was very active in his life. I knew that Zachary would need a man around to help me guide him in areas, whereas a mom, I just wouldn't be enough for a boy. They'd go fishing, skating, to the movies, out to dinner. They spent time together to just talk about life.

Lincoln idolized his older brother Zachary. He wanted to do everything that his brother did. So, although he was little, he acted more like a teenager because he was always hanging out with his older brother.

There were moments I found Zachary and Kait struggling academically, but it was only because they found it difficult to keep themselves engaged with the small things. Zachary always did extremely well when it came to tests. But when it came to completing homework assignments and extra projects, he'd lose focus.

Because of everything that happened early in their childhood, the kids and I pretty much talked about everything. Some people may have even deemed our conversations to be inappropriate at times, but truthfully, I made it my goal to be available no matter the topic. It was so important, given the circumstances we had lived through, that the kids felt comfortable to openly talk with me about drugs, sex, or whatever others topics might cross their minds. Unfortunately, the open conversations seemed to work better with Zachary than Kait. It wasn't her fault. She had been taught at a very young age to bottle up her feelings, and at times to be sneaky- traits that I saw her carry through into her preteen and teen years.

Eventually, at the prompting of a friend, I started an online dating profile. I went on a couple of dates, but those guys were only interested in one thing. I had no intentions of getting into a serious relationship. Honestly, I was terrified that I would end up in yet another toxic relationship. Right as I was at the point of saying, "Screw dating," I received a message from a guy named Jonathan, saying he had recently gotten divorced and was looking for friendship. He asked me if I'd like to go out for good conversation, food, and drinks. His message seemed very genuine, and I accepted his offer. He took me to dinner to a delicious Mexican restaurant on our first date. We planned to go to a bar afterward, but instead, sat in his car in the restaurant parking lot, talking for hours, and what impressed me most, was that one of the topics of conversation was religion. It's not too often that you meet someone for the first time and talk about God.

As time went by, our friendship slowly evolved into a romance, and Jonathan altered my entire outlook on relationships. He was the first guy in my life that taught me what it was like to be in a relationship where there was trust and communication. I had gone through so many toxic relationships that it was almost unbelievable to find a normal relationship. As crazy as it may sound, I struggled with the lack of toxicity at the beginning of our relationship. When I would tell him that I was going to hang out with some friends, I wasn't bombarded with questions. There was no interrogation of, "Who will you be with? Where are you going? What are you doing? How long will you be out?"

I remember thinking, "Man, does this guy even care about me? Why hasn't he checked on me at all?"

Never once did it cross my mind that *this* was real love, and what I had experienced up to this point were control and manipulation. He taught me that it was okay and acceptable to be my own person. I didn't need to conform myself to be everything that I thought he wanted me to be, nor did I need to give up everything that made me who I was for him. I could be me, he could be himself, and we could both be happy and in love. This was how a "normal" relationship worked. I giggle as I write this because, "Wow, what a change! I could NEVER go back to being smothered. There's nothing like appreciating my own personal space and having trust in a relationship."

As an amazing bonus, he also had three kids of his own, very close in age to my kids. Although we didn't live together, we eventually became a beautiful blended family, always hanging out together. Anthony was his oldest, only a few years older than Kait. Haile and my daughter are only one year apart, and Liam, his youngest, only a year and a half older than Lincoln. Zach was the middle child, but believe it or not, he was easily adaptable to whichever kid he happened to be hanging out with. Their closeness in age allowed them all to become close to each other. They were like siblings. Throughout the years, we took the kids on super fun family trips. His daughter and I built a special bond, and she became like my own. Not that the boys were any different, I easily grew to love them as well, but she and I were pretty close, and at times even when I planned vacations for my kids and me, I'd get to bring her along. We visited places as a family, like Disney World, an absolute must when your mom was raised in Florida. We also enjoyed camping, concerts, beaches, and places like Indiana Dunes.

Life was finally great. I had a good career, a beautiful home, the kids had stability, but I couldn't have ever imagined what the next chapter of our lives would bring.

Chapter 13

This Is Your Father

If you plan to have open conversations with your children, I would warn you to brace yourself. Although I offered open conversations, Kait still kept some things guarded. Zachary, however, was really open with me about his friends and relationships. He had no filter, as most would when talking to their mother about their escapades, but I always listened and tried to offer him the best advice I could. All throughout middle school, he was a little heartthrob. I'm sure that was what contributed to him always having a girlfriend. I would constantly tell him to be safe and have fun. But quickly remind him that he shouldn't get too serious because there was no way he was getting married at his age.

Other than girls, another topic of interest seemed to be his father. My ex-husband's parents still had communication with the kids on and off, they'd call the kids on their birthdays or on holidays, and sometimes sent presents. When Zachary was ten years old, he snuck behind my back and created an email account to talk to his dad. Their grandma had snuck a letter from their father, and he had included his email address for them to "contact him" if they wanted to, and so that's exactly what Zach did.

I was always honest with my children about who their father was and the things he had done. Zach was too little to remember everything that happened, but he was aware of the abuse we all endured. Some things that the kids didn't remember I chose to leave out because I felt they were not old enough to hear. Deep down, I knew that one day there would come a point in their lives when they might want a relationship with him. After all, he was their father. I always told myself I would have to back them up on that, but knew I didn't have too much to worry about since they were not allowed to have unsupervised visits until they were sixteen.

When I found out that Zachary had been in contact with his father via email behind my back, I allowed Zachary to play Call of Duty with him online. I was always in the room, able to hear everything that they were talking about, but it was still nerve-racking, knowing that my son wanted a relationship with him. After a while, he began blowing Zachary off. He always had something else that he needed to do, so eventually, Zachary gave up. He was tired of pursuing a relationship with someone who wouldn't pursue him back.

I hoped that might be the end of it, but knew deep down that he'd probably want to reach out again sooner or later.

When Zach was 12 and Kait was 14, Jonathan and I took all the kids to Florida. I wanted them to see my family and their grandparents. Despite the things that happened with my ex, I always tried to be fair to the grandparents as I realized I should not fault them for the terrible things their son had done to us. There were a few instances where my ex-mother-in-law had gone behind my back and sent communication to the kids from their father, as I mentioned before, and we'd have heated arguments over it. As a result, I'd cut off all communication to protect the kids, but I did realize that she loved her grandchildren, and she also loved her son, so in her mind, she was probably only doing what she thought was "right." I honestly had zero trust. Zachary had gone behind my back and asked his grandmother to see his father. Thankfully, she was trying to re-establish a relationship with me as she had not seen the kids in quite some time. I must give her credit for being nice enough to tell me despite our differences. I still, to this day, appreciate her offering me that respect.

I talked to Zach about it, and he told me, "I want to see my dad in person. I want to know what he is like."

I had to make the hardest decision of my life at that very moment for my son. I never wanted to see the man again after what he had done to my kids. But I knew if Zachary wanted to meet his father, I had to be supportive. I was stuck between a rock and a hard place! My daughter, who wanted nothing to do with him, rightfully so, my son, who was desperately searching for that father figure, and my own feelings all very conflicting…ugh! It was tough! I spoke to Kait privately and asked her how she'd feel if her brother went to see their father. She at first questioned it and was extremely angry towards her brother, but I calmly explained to her the different mindsets, and I knew that if I didn't take him, he'd eventually find a way.

She said, "I don't care as long as I never have to see him again or hear about him."

I asked his mother for his phone number as it had been years since I had spoken to him. The last conversation we had was a screaming match about him molesting our daughter, which of course, he denied. Having his number in my hand instantly made me sick to my stomach. I had to remind myself I was doing this for Zachary. I needed him to see for himself who his father was since he was clearly curious.

I texted my ex-husband: *Your son wants to see you.* He responded back with his address, and we set a time to meet the next day. I was sick to my stomach from that moment on. We spent the morning at Universal Studios, and then dropped Kait off with my family. My boyfriend decided that this was something I shouldn't do alone, so he decided to drive us.

On our way there, I got a phone call from him confirming that we were still going to meet. Once I told him we were on our way, he asked if I would partake in smoking weed with him. He thought this might lessen the tension.

"Not with my child." I snapped, "No!" and hung up.

I remember thinking, "Who the fuck hasn't seen their child in years and thinks getting high is a good way to ease the tension?"

It probably wasn't the right thing to do, but I looked at Zachary sitting in the backseat and told him I didn't want him to have any expectations on what might happen.

We pulled up to this big blue house with white trim, and I thought, "Wow, this is where he lives?" I sent him a text "here" and waited for him to come outside. All those arguments that we had over moving out of the trailer park and now he lives in this big blue house.

Zachary pulled me from my thoughts, "Mom, he's outside."

I looked out my window and didn't see anyone standing outside. "Where? I don't see him."

Zachary leaned into the front seat and pointed, "Over there."

To the left of the house, there was an old mobile home. It was very eerie-looking, or maybe I just felt that way knowing he lived there. Sure enough, there he was, standing with his wife waving at us. We were in the wrong driveway. We backed out and drove up to the driveway where they were standing, and Zachary got out of the car. His dad walked right up to him and began to cry as he hugged him. I hardly recognized him. He looked older, with a long beard down to his chest, and a mohawk. Nothing like the well-groomed, clean-cut guy I remembered. Seeing him hold Zachary flooded my mind with all the abuse and torment he had put the kids through. I became very emotional and began shaking. Once again, I stayed calm and kept it together for Zachary's sake.

They awkwardly asked if we wanted to go get food, but we said we weren't really hungry. Then he walked up to my boyfriend, extended his arm out, and introduced himself. Jonathan, honestly, the most polite person I know, responded, "No offense, man, but I'm not shaking your hand."

I was shocked. As my ex walked away, I glanced at my boyfriend. He leaned over and whispered, "That was for Kait."

They invited us inside, and we followed. The place was very old-looking and smelled of mothballs. To the right of the door was a computer desk, a recliner, a couch, and a coffee table. To the left was a small dining room table in the kitchen. They invited us to sit down so we could talk. His wife sat on the recliner chair, he sat on a computer chair by his desk, and Zach and I sat on the couch. My boyfriend sat at one of the dining room table chairs facing the door. He was like our bodyguard in case anything went down.

The entire time, my ex showed Zachary replays of *Call of Duty*, a game that Zach enjoyed playing. I'm not sure if he was trying to make things relatable or what his plan was with all the video game talk. He tried asking me a few questions. I honestly couldn't tell you what they were because seeing him made me very uncomfortable. His wife stared at Zachary and I with tears. I never quite figured that out.

The entire time, he talked about himself, how he didn't have a job, and spent most of his time playing his video games. Zachary squeezed my hand a few times and would ask, "Are you okay, Mom?"

At first, I thought he could sense my tension of being in his father's presence, but after a few more squeezes, I picked up on the queue. He was ready to leave, but didn't want to say that in front of his father. I told them that we had to get going, and we walked out to the car. When we shut the doors, Zachary sat in the back seat super quiet. We were all quiet for a moment as my boyfriend backed out of the driveway.

"He didn't even ask me about my life," Zachary said, breaking the silence, "I don't want to talk to him or see him again."

The next day, his dad texted me, asking me why Zachary wasn't answering his calls. I told him what Zach had said and asked him to respect his son's decision. As most conversations went with my ex, things got heated, and nothing went well. I ended up having to change Zach's number so he would leave him alone.

There was a sense of relief that Zach didn't want to see his dad. Kait had already expressed that she never wanted to see or hear of her father again. Now that Zachary was able to see him for himself, I hoped that we could close that door for good.

Although he shrugged it off as never wanting to see his father again, the whole encounter must have cut much deeper. During seventh grade, he mentioned to a counselor that he wanted to die. The counselor had him evaluated further to determine if Zachary might be a threat to himself. It was determined that he was not a threat to himself, and the comment was nothing more than a comment.

Around eighth grade, Zachary really started to find himself. He had a ton of friends. Pretty much every weekend, he'd have sleepovers at our house, and the boys would do crazy boy things, like take mattresses out in the yard to learn how to do backflips. Zach loved to do backflips and would practice for hours. When he wasn't with his friends, he was out exploring the neighborhood on his bicycle, skateboarding, or playing the piano.

When we were in Florida visiting my mom, he started playing her keyboard and loved it. So, for his 13th birthday, all he wanted was a piano. I found an old piano on Craigslist and surprised him. Little did I know, I'd be the one surprised. Typically, he never really stuck to any hobbies, but piano was much different. Playing on the piano came naturally, and he would literally play for hours. Within a year, he had taught himself to play anything, from Mozart to new-age music, like 21 Pilots. I was super proud of him, and admired his dedication. However, having a piano play nonstop in the house can start to wear on the nerves. Eventually, I bought him a keyboard and headphones so that he could play without the entire house having to listen to the music.

Chapter 14

The Struggle with Zachary

When I dreamed of having a baby boy, I never thought of the challenges that might accompany him. Zachary was always the happiest kid to be around. He was extremely loving, but also very impulsive. He would do things without a single thought to the consequences. It was never anything horrible, normal things that boys might get into, but as he got older, the choices began to change, and with that, he began to change as well. I wasn't quite sure how to handle it. No one ever hands you a user manual on your kids. Each of them is different, so there's not a one-way approach to handling situations. A lot of it is as it comes up.

The summer before he started his freshman year, I came home from work, and Zachary told me he needed to talk to me. He said, "Mom, I have to tell you something. I had sex with this girl, but I feel kinda bad because I think it was a dumb choice. I'm not ready for all that, so I want to dump her."

I told him that he needed to be careful because once you have sex with a girl, they can get super emotionally attached. Little did he know, I was speaking from personal experiences. I let him know emotions could also make girls a little crazy. He needed to let her down easy.

I had no idea how right I would be. When he broke up with her, rumors started spreading around the school that he had sexually assaulted this girl. I didn't find out until much later that kids around the school were threatening to beat him up. He even ended up losing his best friend over it.

Everything was finally brought to my attention when I pulled up to the high school to pick up the kids after a football game. Kait got into the car and said, "You tell Mom or I will."

I looked at the two of them with confusion. "Tell me what?"

Zachary slouched down in the back seat and stared out the window. "You tell her."

Kait began telling me that she had been cornered by a group of mean girls during the football game. They got into a huge argument because the girls accused Zachary of being a rapist. At some point, she got in between a six-foot-tall kid and Zach because the kid was trying to beat Zachary up.

I was shocked to hear about the event, but even more shocked that Zachary had been living through this for a while without me hearing about it. I was furious that he was going through this at school. But at the same time, I wasn't sure how we should handle the situation. I explained that we could get the authorities or school administration involved, but doing so could potentially lead to Zachary being labeled as a sex offender for the rest of his life. I wanted to stop this girl from making false accusations, but

I didn't want to make things potentially worse. I asked Zach and Kait if I should go to the school to make this stop.

Zach immediately said, "NO! If you go to the school, things will only get worse for me"

So, I didn't. Looking back, that is where a lot of things began to change. Zachary began going through sudden bursts of anger and sadness. I thought for sure it must be due to the hormonal changes of puberty. But I also knew that some of it had to be what he was experiencing at school. Whatever it was, the Zachary I knew was changing.

A few weeks later, there was another football game. Kait had a volleyball game away, and Zachary decided to attend the football game alone. When I pulled up to the high school after the football game to pick him up, he was sitting in front of the school waiting for me.

The moment he got into the car, I knew something was off. It didn't take me long to determine that he was higher than a kite. I became irate. I had made so many poor choices with drugs that I couldn't imagine my baby boy making the same mistakes.

"Zach, are you high?"

"No, Mom," he sighed, "of course not."

"Zachary, do NOT lie to me. I've always told you lying will only make things worse. Tell me the truth right now."

"Okay," he ran his hands through his fluffy hair, "yes, I smoked weed with a friend."

The questions flooded through my mind and spilled out of my mouth. "What? Where? When?"

"We left campus and went to a guy's house. I smoked a lot," he chuckled as he continued messing with his hair.

"Zachary, this is serious." I panicked at his lack of concern, "Do you realize that this can potentially lead you to harder drugs? Do you understand that if you decide to pick up a crack pipe or try heroin, those are drugs that you'll never come back from? And what about the dangers, and potentially overdosing?"

There were so many things that I wanted him to know. I wanted to ensure that he never wanted to try drugs again. As I talked, I could see the dazed look in his eyes. I had never seen his beautiful green eyes look so empty. I felt terrible, and at the same time was in shock. At that moment, I realized he was truly super high. Nothing I was saying was actually registering in his mind. I shut off the lecturing mom mode for a moment. High or not, I loved him and wanted him to know I loved him. In that moment, I did what any best friend of a pothead might do. I drove to McDonald's.

"I'm sure you have the munchies. What do you want?" I asked as I pulled up to the speaker.

"Four cheeseburgers and two McChickens."

I laughed as I placed the order. We got the food. As he ate, I turned the car radio up and we "car" danced while he ate his food. We drove back to the school to wait for Kaitlynn to return from her volleyball game.

The next day, we calmly talked about the dangers of drugs and I grounded him. I took his cell phone away and made him watch a ton of YouTube videos about addiction & STDs with me. He was super annoyed, but sat there and watched them all. I really wasn't trying to torture him. I just wanted to show him drug addiction was real. I wanted him to understand that most people started out by smoking weed before moving on to heavier drugs. We watched videos about overdosing. At this point, he thought I was overreacting and being ridiculous, but he continued watching them. I just wanted him to understand the effects that drugs have on people.

That night, Zach came in my room and hugged me. Of the three kids, he was always the one who would come to my room every night and say, "I love you, Mom." He was super affectionate in that way. That night, it was just a hug. He'd get in trouble, I'd be a hard ass, but his silent hugs always confirmed that he knew I meant well.

Chapter 15-

I Don't Even Know Who You Are

Two weeks into high school, Zachary had to have his wisdom teeth removed. Since I had just started a new job, I couldn't take any time off, so my boyfriend took him to surgery. The doctor recommended that Zachary stay home from school for a week after the surgery. However, Zachary didn't want to miss school, so he had surgery on Friday and returned to school the following Monday.

On Wednesday, I received a phone call from school stating that Zachary was not there. I repeatedly called his phone with no answer; when I got home from work, something was off. For Kait's 16th birthday, I had given her a car, but because she didn't officially have her license yet, the car stayed parked in our driveway. Although the car didn't appear to have been moved, I had this crazy inkling that he had taken the car.

Granted, he had been making one poor decision after another recently, but he was only fourteen. Why would he attempt to drive the car? I shrugged off the strange feeling and walked into the house. "Why aren't you at school?"

"I missed the bus, so I decided to stay home. My teeth were hurting."

He response was so emotionless. It infuriated me. Any other time he had ever missed the bus, he would always call me to tell me. He never ever just stayed home. So, I yelled at him for skipping school. The scolding didn't seem to phase him in the least. I felt like I was at my wits end with him because it was beginning to be one bad decision after another. I was terrified that in some way, he would end up getting in trouble with the law, and I did the unthinkable.

I called his father. It had been a couple years since our awkward living room visitation. Other than that, we hadn't spoken to each other.

He answered the phone, and I explained why I was calling.

"Look, I'm calling you because I need you to talk to our son. I need you to tell him what it was like going to prison at 17. I'm scared that he's going to get himself into trouble that I won't be able to get him out of."

His dad was irate and started yelling at me for wanting to use him as a bad example for our son; I told him I wasn't trying to use him as a bad example. I wanted Zachary to understand that his actions could have bad consequences. He spoke to him on the speaker phone for 3 hours, but the conversation didn't go as I planned it to go. By the end of the conversation, his father said,

"It seems to me that your mother can't handle you, so why don't you come live with me?"

I was livid. What an asshole! I hung up the phone and continued arguing with Zachary about the choices he had been making. He went to his room, and I sat down on my bed, trying to process everything.

Around that time, Lincoln ran into my room crying. "I'm so sorry, Mom."

Confused I said "For what?"

"For letting Zachary take the car today." He cried, "I told him no, but he wouldn't listen to me."

"Whatttt?? Where did he take the car?"

"After school, he told me to get in, and we drove around and went to McDonald's."

The fuse had been relit. I was furious. I went to Zachary's room with all that rage boiling inside of me. "What are you? A psychopath or a sociopath? You endangered your life, and not only that, your brother's life too. You're fourteen. You don't even know how to drive! You went through a very dangerous intersection."

Zachary began to cry and say, "I just don't think about consequences. When I want to do something, I just do it."

Although I was super upset, I instantly regretted my reaction. Unfortunately, I couldn't take it back.

The next day, Haile called me at work. She was crying, "You need to go pick up Zachary right now. He says he'd be better off dead because you called him a psychopath. Please go pick him up, he's crying hysterically, and I'm worried."

I told my boss I had an emergency and immediately went to sign Zachary out of school. When I picked him up, he told me he had a headache. We drove to Walgreens, and I went in to buy headache pills. When I came back out, he told me he didn't want to talk about it.

"Zachary, I am sorry for saying that to you. I was just angry, and it's no excuse. I don't think that you're a psychopath or a sociopath. You're smart and just have to make better choices. I love you, and I just want you to please tell me what's going on." I pleaded with him to talk to me.

He finally told me that he did say he wanted to die. But he was just upset and felt better now. I looked at my son while we sat in my car. I held his hand. That was our thing. We'd often hold hands in the car. In that moment, I began to think of what life might be like if he was no longer there to hold my hand. "Zachary if anything ever happened to you…I'd be destroyed. Please understand that I could never live my life without you."

"Mom, I was just upset, I feel a lot better now."

Regardless of whether or not he felt better now, I couldn't help remember him saying the same thing two years earlier after meeting his father for the first time. Now, here we were in ninth grade, facing the same kind of talk. I immediately signed him up for counseling, but with the waiting list, it would be a little while before he started.

In the meantime, my new job was sponsoring a suicide awareness walk. Because Zachary had recently made the comment that he wanted to die, I thought the event would be a good thing for us to attend. It was September 15th, 2018. We had to be there pretty early to register, so I woke Zachary up and asked him to get dressed. He didn't want to listen and told me he didn't feel like going to this walk. I told him I thought it would be good for him and he argued with me about going. My boyfriend was also planning to attend the event, so I called him to see if he could talk Zachary into going.

After talking with him, Zachary got dressed. Although he seemed annoyed the entire ride to the event, once we arrived, he turned into the cheery kid he once had been. Kait had spent the night at a friend's house, so it was just me and the boys. My boyfriend and his three kids met us there. After we registered for the walk and bought the kids t-shirts, we decided to check out the sponsors. Businesses had set up tents and stations. Some of the stations had games where the kids could play and win prizes. Some of the prizes included packs of gum or other types of candy, but one booth had coupons for free cheesy fries from

Beef-a-Roo, a local restaurant. Liam, Lincoln, and Zachary must have played 10 rounds each!

We had brought our dog, Oso, a Rottweiler pup, with us. Zach was running around with him, interacting with all kinds of people before the walk began. As we stood in line to start the walk, I took pictures of the kids waiting in line with the dog. I never would have guessed by the smiles that Zach hadn't wanted to come.

Once the walk started, Zachary and I were walking next to each other with Oso. The walk was along a path next to Rock River. Although it was hot and humid, it was still a beautiful morning. The water flowing down the river was peaceful and refreshing. Suddenly, the mood turned sad as I noticed a woman in front of us sobbing. Another lady walking next to her was rubbing her back to comfort her. I pulling Zachary close to my side, and hugging him, locked my eyes into his beautiful green eyes, "Do you see how distraught that lady is? She clearly lost someone to suicide and is heartbroken. That would be me if anything ever happened to you, you realize that, right?"

He put his arm around me and pulled me close for a side hug as we walked. He smiled at me with that beautifully contagious smile of his, "Mom, I'd never do anything like that. Don't worry."

We continued to the end of the walk. As we were leaving, Lincoln decided to go with Jonathan and his kids. On our way home, since it was just the two of us, Zachary asked if we could go to

Beef-a-Roo. He wanted to cash in some of the free cheese fries coupons.

While we were at Beef-a-Roo, he ordered a cheese burger and cheddar fries. I had a buffalo wrap and cheddar fries as well. Our mother/son date at Beef-a-Roo was an unexpected break from the arguments and tension we'd experienced the past few days. He sat across from me, and we had an amazing conversation. I asked him why he had started smoking pot and if it made him paranoid.

He said, "No way, I feel super relaxed when I do it. I don't have to think about anything. I just sit back and relax."

Thankfully, I was able to tell him my concerns. He was only fourteen. I just wanted him to understand the dangers of drugs. He listened to my concerns and assured me that he understood I was looking out for him. It was a great conversation, and we talked and laughed for quite a while.

After Beef-a-Roo, we went back to our house. Zachary had signed up for the Powder Puff team at school. For this event, girls dressed up as football players and go on the field to play while the guys dress up as cheerleaders and cheer from the sidelines. All the guys that had signed up were coming over to the house to practice. I sat in the backyard, watching and taking videos as this goofy group of teenage boys tried to learn a dance routine. Zachary was all into it. He would crack up when they had to do silly jumps. But he was getting the routine down and helping teach the other boys. I had fun watching them.

Later in the evening, I had made plans for dinner with a friend. All the kids went to my boyfriend's house to hang out. Before dinner, I stopped over there to check on everybody and kill some time. When I walked in, Zachary said, "Mom, you look beautiful." I appreciated his thoughtfulness. It was always in those moments that all the bad choices he had made seemed to melt away. At least I knew that my thoughtful, sweet, innocent little boy was still in there somewhere.

As I was leaving, Zachary followed me outside and said, "Mom, have fun tonight, but please be safe. I worry about you."

I thought it was a little strange for my fourteen-year-old to worry about me. I smiled and asked, "Why do you worry?"

And he said, "Not sure, I just worry, please just be safe." He gave me a really tight bear hug, looked at me, and hugged me once more. "I love you, Mom."

"I love you, Zach."

As I got in my car and watched him go back in the house, I felt a super uneasy feeling rush over me. I felt as if that would be the last time I would ever hug my son. I shrugged it off as something awful but not true. Then I backed out of the driveway and proceeded with my plans.

Chapter 16

When It Rains...

A few weeks back, I had put an offer on my dream home: a five-acre farm. I wanted to make some extra cash for the down payment in case they'd accept my offer. My boyfriend offered to give me cash if I cleaned his house and did his laundry. Sounded like a plan to me.

The day after the suicide awareness walk, I woke up early. Lincoln and I were heading to my boyfriend's house to do some cleaning. Kait and Zachary were still asleep. It was a beautiful morning; the weather was perfect and sunny! Lincoln played video games as I cleaned. After a little while, my phone rang, it was Zachary, asking where we were. I told him and asked him to please clean his room and do chores around the house.

He said, "Okay." I hung up and went back to scrubbing Jonathan's stove. His phone rang. I heard him answer it, but continued scrubbing away, until I heard him say, "Oh, my God!" I looked over at him, the blood had drained from his face. He looked like someone had punched him in the gut. His dad was on the other end, letting him know that his cousin had passed away early that morning in a tragic accident.

The news was saddening and shocked us. We needed more details before we could plan to attend a funeral, so we tried to continue about our day. Around one that afternoon, I got a phone call from my aunt. The farmhouse was having one last open house before the owners made their decision on whether they'd accept my offer. She wanted to meet me at the house so she could walk around and see if maybe she or her boyfriend could notice anything concerning. We met at the farm a few hours later and did the walkthrough. My aunt had no concerns. Nerves were killing me because the new job I had required me to move to the city that I was working in. This was the only property in the city that would allow me to have our horse on our property. This job was the kind of place I could see myself retiring from, so I needed this home to be approved.

The open house ended at 5:00 pm. Shortly after, I was given the news that the owners would accept my offer. This was going to be our home! I needed to give the realtor the earnest money and sign the contract to move forward with the sale.

Despite the sad news of my boyfriend's cousin's passing that morning, I was thrilled with this news. I called Kait and Zach and gave them the big news over the phone. I told them I'd pick up fast food for dinner. They both told me what they wanted me to pick up, and we hung up the phone. Lincoln and I picked up Taco Bell and went home.

A friend was meeting me at the house. He was going to drive back out to this five-acre farmhouse that would soon be mine. The realtor was going to meet us there with the contract.

Lincoln decided he wanted to stay home with Kait and Zach. Right as I was leaving, Zachary came running downstairs, "Mom, Mom, Mom, can I go to the football field at the high school to hang out with a few friends?"

"No, I don't think you need to. It's going to be dark soon." It was a Sunday evening and I really didn't want him out with friends. I was afraid he would just go get himself into trouble if he went out.

He became really upset and raised his voice, "I CLEANED MY ROOM, I DID MY CHORES, WHY CAN'T I GO?"

"Zach, I'm not arguing about this right now." I grabbed my purse and keys, "I really have to go. It's just not a good idea."

"THIS IS SO STUPID, WHY CAN'T I GO?"

Kait was in the kitchen. She came around the corner, "Zach, stop yelling at Mom, do you really think you deserve to go anywhere? You've been skipping school, smoking weed, you stole Mom's car, you shouldn't go anywhere!"

He started running up the stairs and stopped halfway. "Why does she get to decide if I go?" he yelled at me. His eyes were narrowed and upset. "This is so dumb!"

"Zach, she's not deciding. I am, but she's right! I will be back soon, just relax."

He went upstairs and slammed his bedroom door. I looked at Kait. "Make sure that you guys eat your dinner, I'll be right back."

My friend was outside waiting in his truck, and we left. We stopped at Chipotle for food, and ran into Zachary's "Big Brother." He asked where Zach was out and how he was doing, we talked a few minutes, then proceeded to the farmhouse. Once we were about to leave the property, I said, "I wonder how far this actually is from my new job."

He said, "It shouldn't be that far. Wanna drive there and see?"

I had an uneasy feeling in my gut. I felt like I needed to get home for whatever reason; it was really odd. But I dismissed the feeling and told my friend that we should see how far it was. It was only going to take me ten minutes to get to work. As we were heading back to the house, my phone rang. Kait was on the other end, crying hysterically.

"Kait, calm down, I can't understand you. What's going on?" The only word I could make out from her hysteria was "Mom" over and over. "Kait, calm down, what's happening?"

In the most horrifying scream, she took a breath and said, "Mom, please come home. Zachary is hanging in his closet, and I can't get him down."

Chapter 17

...It Pours

I immediately screamed, "NO, NO, NO, NO! This can't be happening." I hung up on Kait and called 911.

"911 Operator, what is your emergency?"

I stated my address, "I need you to please get emergency personnel to my house immediately. My children are home alone, and my daughter just called me to tell me that my son is hanging in the closet. PLEASE, I need help!"

"How old is your son, ma'am?" the woman asked calmly.

"He's 14, PLEASE." I begged, trying to compose myself.

"Is he breathing?"

"I don't know. I'm not there. Please, I'm on my way, I need you to get an ambulance there right away."

"Okay, ma'am, stay on the phone with me."

"No, I'm sorry. I have to go, my three kids are home alone, please, just send help!"

I disconnected with 911 and tried calling Kait back. The phone rang over and over, but she never answered. Suddenly, to my surprise, Jonathan called me. I picked up the phone and screamed, "Kait just called me. Please get over there. Zachary is hanging in the closet, and I need someone to get him down."

He replied, "I know, I just got a phone call from my ex's husband."

His ex-wife and her husband lived in the same neighborhood as me and the kids. For whatever strange reason, they had decided to stop at my house. I didn't really have a relationship of any kind with them, so to me, how this happened is shocking. When she walked up to the house, she heard Lincoln screaming, so she walked inside to make sure everything was ok. She thought maybe Kait and Zach were picking on him. But when she walked in and realized what was happening, she quickly ran upstairs to help Kait try to get Zach down. Even with both of them, they still were not strong enough to get him down. Her husband stayed downstairs to call my boyfriend.

We were stuck at a traffic light right before the house. I could hear tons of sirens. An ambulance and three squad cars sped down the road to my house. I screamed at my friend to run the red light and get to the house. We ended up pulling up to the house right as the ambulance and cop cars pulled in. I jumped out of the truck as it rolled to a stop. I ran up the hill of my front yard and burst into the house. "Is he okay? Please tell me, he's okay?"

The paramedics and some of the officers had rushed upstairs. My boyfriend's ex-wife stood at the bottom of the stairs guarding the walk-up. "No, you're not going up there." I begged her to please move out of the way and let me go upstairs, and she said sternly "No, you're not going up there, I'm not letting you see him like this." She called for her husband and asked him to take me outside. It seemed like an eternity passed by as I stood out front with him, crying.

Lincoln came outside. I sat down on the front porch bench with him. He sat on my lap, holding me, trying to calm me down in the midst of his crying as he said, "It's okay, Mommy. Zachary is going to be okay; he's okay."

The cops asked me to come back inside; they needed information. I sat Lincoln on the bench and told him I'd be right back. He sat there alone, crying. The cops were asking me questions "Where were you? How old are the kids? What happened?"

I don't really remember all the questions as I was focused on wanting to know if my son was alive. Everything began to blur. This all had to be a horrible nightmare. It was time for me to wake up and end these awful events, but unfortunately that never happened. No one would tell me anything. I just wanted to know if my son was going to be ok.

At some point, my boyfriend showed up. I'm not sure how long it had been, but I was still waiting for them to tell me if my son was okay. No one would let me go upstairs. I can't even tell you how long they were up there, but it seemed like hours. Finally, they brought Zachary downstairs on a stretcher; his eyes were halfway open, his face was completely purple. They had an oxygen mask on him, and one of the paramedics was squeezing the plastic bottle attached to the mask.

For a moment, I had hope that he was ok. They were feeding him air, so that must be a good sign. I rushed outside as the paramedics rolled him on the stretcher towards the ambulance. "Is he okay? Is he alive?"

A paramedic replied, "We're taking him to the hospital."

I asked if I could ride in the ambulance, and they apologized but said I could not. They loaded him into the ambulance and took off for the hospital.

I asked my boyfriend to call Lincoln's father to come pick him up. I wasn't sure how long we'd be at the hospital. His ex-wife and husband stayed with Kait and his kids at my house. My boyfriend drove me to the hospital. As soon as we entered the emergency room, I told them who we were. A nurse came out and asked if we were the parents of the kid who was just brought in, then took us back to a room filled with nurses.

They had a machine hooked up to his chest, doing compressions. The doctor, a tall oriental guy, walked right up to me and asked, "Are you 'Mom'? I just want you to know that I'm doing the best I can, but I really need you to prepare for the worst."

Prepare for the worst? No mother wants to hear that when her child is lying on a hospital bed. I walked up to Zachary. The lifeless expression in his eyes told me that he was already gone.

The doctor finally directed everyone to stop. He looked at me. "I'm so sorry, there is nothing more that we can do." He turned to his nursing staff. "Time of death: 7:34."

I held my son's hand. He was gone. I kissed him and cried. His beautiful green eyes weren't the same. My boyfriend had his arms around my shoulder. They brought us chairs. I sat next to my son as people walked in and out of the room. I asked the nurses if they could remove the tube from his throat, but it was a while before they actually took it out. A priest came into the room and prayed over Zachary at one point. He even brought me an ibuprofen because I had a terrible headache. Nurses walked in and out of the room, but I didn't want to leave him. I didn't want to let go of his hand. It was our thing, holding hands, and this would be the last time I'd get to hold his.

At some point, my boyfriend's ex-wife and her husband brought Kait and Haile to the hospital. As they walked in through the automatic double doors of the emergency room, his ex-wife looked at Jonathan as he shook his head to indicate Zach didn't make it. The girls asked if Zachary was okay as Jonathan walked to them, "I'm sorry, Zach's gone." There was a yipping cry from Kait. Just a single squeal. We walked into a separate room with them and the priest. The priest comforted us and prayed the Lord's Prayer. The girls were crying. For whatever reason, I realized that I should call Zachary's father and let him know. As soon as I told him what had happened, he started yelling at me. I don't remember what all he had said because Kait took the phone from my hand in the middle of the yelling.

"You need to calm down. You do not get to yell at my mother. She's the only parent we've ever had, and her son just died." She yelled back and then hung up.

I also called Zachary's "Big Brother" from the hospital. He said something along the lines of, "What?" and "Oh, my God." But I don't remember much more from our conversation.

I went back into the room with Zachary and sat alone with him while Jonathan called my family to give them the devastating news. I rubbed Zachary's hair and face. I laid my head on his chest and told him how much I love him. I was distraught. I looked into his beautiful eyes, which were now lifeless and unrecognizable.

My ex-husband called back, "Please tell me this is some sick joke, and it's not true."

"I am so sorry, I wish it was."

"Can you please put me on speaker phone and put the phone next to him so he can hear me?" I did as he asked, and proceeded to listen as he spoke to our dead child, "I am so, so sorry, baby boy, I'm so sorry for everything I ever did." Then he proceeded to tell me he would try to come up, but finances were tight and needed to speak to his parents to figure it all out.

Unfortunately, this is where my storytelling gets a little bit jumbled. It's hard to recall events that you'd much rather forget. Hard to relive the pain of such horrible memories. I held Zach's hand until rigor mortis started to take place. My boyfriend literally had to pry off his fingers from in between mine. Having to say goodbye to him at the hospital was the worst pain I ever had to endure.

I felt as if part of me had died with my son that night.

Chapter 18

Mom, Listen to Me

After leaving the hospital, Jonathan drove me back to his house. Kait and Haile followed us home in a separate car. They went in his daughter's room to lay down. I laid on my boyfriend's lap on his couch, uncontrollably crying. I kept saying "No, God, no. This isn't real. No, my baby, why?"

Suddenly, as if telepathically, I started hearing Zachary's voice in my mind, "Mom, it's okay. I'm so sorry, Mom. Please don't cry, Mom. I'm okay, I'm okay, Mom."

I sobbed harder. "I've literally lost my damn mind. I can hear Zachary's voice telling me that he's okay."

My boyfriend might have said something back, I can't remember, because right after I told him I heard Zachary, my son started speaking again.

"Mom, please listen to me, you have to get up and go in the other room. You have to tell Kait that this is not her fault."

I sat up on the couch and said, "I'm going crazy. He's telling me to go tell Kait it's not her fault."

My boyfriend ran his hand across my back and shrugged. "Just go with it, you're not crazy, go tell her."

We got up and walked into his daughter's bedroom. Both of the girls were lying in his daughter's bed, crying. I walked over and sat down on the edge of the bed. "Kait, I know this is going to sound really crazy, but I can hear your brother talking to me right now. He wanted me to come in here and tell you this isn't your fault."

Kait sobbed. "You're just saying that to make me feel better."

Haile wiped her face, "She's lying in here blaming herself."

Zach spoke again. "Mom, please tell her it's not her fault. Tell her that when they were driving home from the hospital, I was jamming out in the back seat of the car with them to XXXTentacion." Then he started to sing a song.

I repeated what he said, including the song he had sang.

Their eyes widened, and they looked at each other. "Wait, how did you know we were listening to that song?" Kait asked.

"Your brother is telling me this, I swear."

Kait wiped her face for a moment. "Can you ask him if he regrets it, if he regrets taking his own life."

Zachary chuckled and replied in this excited voice. "If you could feel what I feel right now, you'd understand."

I relayed the message to Kait.

114

He proceeded to say, "I love you guys so much," and then I heard his amazing laugh, and in an extremely excited voice, he said, "Mom, Mom, Mom," as he often did when he was excited, "by the way, I finally met Grandma Lynn, she's here with me right now."

For the first time since she died when I was sixteen, I heard Grandma Lynn's voice, "It's okay, Laura, I have your baby boy with me."

At that point, I broke down crying. I was overwhelmed with despair and yet felt so much peace, knowing that Zach was in such loving hands.

"Mom, when you're ready, in my closet on the shelf to the left, there is a black notebook. Next to the notebook, there is a note that you can read whenever you're ready. I'm sorry, Mom, but I have to go, Grandma Lynn says we have to go."

And just like that, I sensed them leaving me – it was the most surreal experience of my life.

Although the conversation had brought me some peace, I literally thought I had lost my damn mind. The next morning, I kept saying to my boyfriend, "I have to be crazy, right?"

He and Haile went over to my house and checked the shelf in Zach's closet. They found a small black notebook, but no letter. My boyfriend came back and handed me the small notebook. "I'm sorry, there's nothing in the notebook about why he did this. And we didn't find a letter next to it."

"See," I replied, "I've lost my mind. I am crazy!"

But after hearing me name off the song our daughters had been listening to the night before, he wasn't quite as convinced. He decided to go back to the house once more. This time, when he returned from the house, he handed me a board. It was about 8x10 in size with stab marks all over it from a sharp knife. "This was right next to the black notebook in Zach's closet, propped up against the wall."

When he handed it to me, I flipped it over, and written in pencil, on the board, the first sentence said, "I have the most amazing mother in the world..."

I could not believe my eyes, but most of all, I couldn't believe that I WAS NOT crazy after all.

Chapter 19

The End of Me

A few hours after his death, I received a phone call, asking from an organ donor agency. They literally asked me a hundred questions about donating his body. I never in my life had considered I would be dealing with the death of one of my children, much less deciding whether or not I should donate their organs. At one point, they asked if I'd be willing to donate Zach's eyes. Thinking about those gorgeous green eyes no longer being on his sweet face really bothered me, but I donated them anyway. Zachary was always the type of child that wanted to help and make a difference for other people. If he had been the one making the decision, he wouldn't have given it a second thought. He'd just go for it.

Jonathan accompanied me to the funeral home to make the arrangement. The strong smell of cleaner and peppermints, as I had to pick out a "package" to lay my child to rest, was overpowering. The cost was beyond shocking. I struggled with the thought of cremating my child; I had this awful image of his body being burnt. I NEVER thought of my child dying, much less what "arrangements" I'd have to make. The tears just rolled down my face as I quietly sat and listened to the long-haired blond lady, sitting across the table, pointing out different options from a paper. Burying him was out of the question, I didn't have the money, so I had to go against my own terrifying thoughts and go with cremation. I don't remember much of the planning after that except that the funeral was scheduled for Friday, September 21, 2018- five days after his death.

Zach's father and his family arrived the day before the funeral. I told his father that I would meet him at the funeral home so we could have a moment alone with our son before the funeral. Before he arrived, I wanted to see Zachary without him. I had not seen my son in four days now. I walked up to the casket. Seeing Zachary lying there made me feel angry. There was the hurt and sadness of losing my child, but whoever had done his hair obviously didn't know who he was. It was all slicked back. Zachary NEVER slicked his hair back. I ran my fingers through his hair to mess it up and give him his usual "floofer-do" as we called it; shaggy, curly, messy mop of hair. That was Zachary. My boyfriend stood behind me the entire time. When he saw Zach in the casket, he fell apart. All he could say was, "Oh, my God!" We both stood there for a moment and cried in disbelief that this was now our reality.

We walked back outside where Zachary's father was standing by a truck, smoking a cigarette. His father and wife sat in the truck as he and I walked into the funeral home together. We stood in front of the casket – alone; just the two of us, with our child's corpse. This time, I didn't feel anything at all when I saw him. I was completely numb. The only thought that was going through my mind was the thought of breaking my promise to my little girl that she would NEVER have to see him again. All I could think about was that this situation was already heartbreaking enough, and breaking my promise to her was devastating, to say the least, under these circumstances. He grabbed my hand, placed it on Zachary's cold hands, and then put his hand on top of mine and cried. I let him have his moment, but at that point, I was filled with disgust. I wanted to scream; I couldn't look at him. I took my hand away and told him I had to leave the room, and as I walked out of that room, he walked behind me, grabbed my arm, and turned my body and said, "Look at me, PLEASE, Laura, LOOK AT ME." I briefly looked into his soulless brown eyes, yanked my arm back, turned and walked away, making my way back outside.

The next day, we held the funeral services.

Jonathan dressed Lincoln in a really sleek blue suit and a pink tie. For a long time, pink was Zach's favorite color. He and Liam walked up to Zachary when we arrived at the funeral home. They just stared at him, lying in the casket. Lincoln did not cry– didn't shed a tear, just stared at his brother's body in shock. Liam stood stiffly next to Lincoln, in front of the person he idolized for so many years of his young life.

Haile, Anthony, and Kait sat together with friends; Anthony was super protective of Kait that day, since we all knew she wanted no part in seeing or talking to her father. It had been 8 years since she had seen his face.

I stood in a black dress in front of my son's casket.

We had poster boards with hundreds of pictures of Zachary displayed around the room. There were beautiful flowers surrounding Zach's casket, and kids had made a banner that week in school for him in his absence during the Powder Puff game that he had been practicing for the day before he passed. We showed a beautiful video, summarizing his life into a four minute and twenty-nine second montage, and played his favorite songs during the visitation.

To my surprise, there were hundreds of kids. The line was so long that it led to the parking lot outside the funeral home. We literally had over five hundred kids sign their name on the funeral memory book. I stood by my son's casket and hugged each and every one of those kids as they passed by to pay their respects; hours and hours of people just coming in and showing support. Kids would go up to Zachary lying in his casket. Some would hug him, some would kiss him, and some would cry on his chest. Others would line up multiple times to hug me and kiss him one more time.

My ex-husband spent most of the funeral outside with his wife, smoking. At some point, he came inside and he asked me if I wanted him to stand next to me by Zachary's casket. "I don't care what you do." As kids walked up and I continued to hug them, he'd say "Hello, I'm Zachary's father." Some kids were polite, shook his hand, some hugged him, but the ones that were close to Zach, no exaggeration when I tell you that some of them would just walk away from him without saying a word as if they knew that he hadn't been a father at all.

We allowed kids to give speeches and tell stories about Zachary. Almost every single girl started her speech with, "I was Zachary's girlfriend." Despite the darkness, it made me laugh. At least he had taken my advice to heart when I told him to have lots of girlfriends rather than get too serious too young. There were also tons of parents who went up to share stories of Zachary staying the night at their homes. He was always super respectful and helpful when he stayed. Boys came forward and talked about what an amazing friend Zach had been.

One of the boys talked about learning how to do his first backflip with Zachary. I looked at him and asked, "Will you do one for Zach?"

The kid smiled super big. "Right now?"

"Yep, right in front of his casket, he wouldn't want it any other way."

The boy ran up to the casket and flipped right next to Zach. Despite the sadness, we all laughed and cried happy tears as we remembered what an amazing kid Zachary was. When kids would get up and start to blame themselves, I would cut them off and redirect them. No one should carry around that kind of guilt. I felt for all of them. I was so overwhelmed and grateful at the stories I heard.

When his bus driver spoke, it touched my soul. She described him exactly to be the kindhearted person that he was. She started off by saying, "Zachary was not like most kids. He enjoyed sitting in the front of the bus in the morning, talking to me. Most kids want to go to the back of the bus, but not Zach. He enjoyed our morning conversations. He always talked very highly of his mother and told me stories about him and his little brother Lincoln. He was nice to every single kid -he was nice to everyone, young or old, and he had a contagious smile."

His family sat together in the front row, but although I should not have been shocked, I was baffled by the lack of respect. Not one of them asked how I was doing. Not one of them said they were sorry for my loss or much of anything. After the service, as they were leaving, my ex-mother-in-law came up to me and said, "I had no idea the kind of life you provided for him." I'm assuming that was a compliment, but otherwise, none of them said anything meaningful and for my son; I was beyond upset. He deserved the world and was a giver.

The unforgettable smell of sadness and heartache embedded itself into my mind that day. As I'm writing this, although it's been almost two years, I'm getting the same nauseating feeling in my stomach. Zach's life ended that day in the hospital, but walking away from that casket for the last time, was as if I left a part of me behind in that room with him.

I felt like that day was the end of me.

Chapter 20

Lincoln's Reenactment

We never returned to our house. I couldn't. It was too painful for me. I basically told Jonathan that until I could close on the farmhouse, I would have to stay at his place. My family had flown up from Florida after I gave them the news of Zach's passing, and I told them apologetically that I just could not go back there, basically pleading for them to deal with it all. Between Jonathan, my mother, stepdad, siblings, and friends, they boxed everything up for me. They packed up my entire house in a matter of 5 days. They left everything ready just to be picked up by movers once I closed on my farmhouse. To this day, I have yet had the emotional strength to go through the boxes with Zach's things in them. They sit neatly in a closet of my farmhouse, waiting until the day I can find the courage to open them. It's honestly painful, even writing about it.

As I said before, Lincoln never cried at the funeral. It was a few weeks before it hit him that Zachary was never coming back. His big brother would never be around to play Fortnite with him, or teach him how to do backflips. Then he proceeded to take me through the occurrences of the night Zachary died, step by step, retold through his six-year-old's point of view.

He told me that after I left, Kait felt bad that Zachary was still in his room and hadn't eaten. She and Lincoln were at the dining room table. Kait called Zachary several times to come downstairs and eat. When he finally came downstairs, all three of them were sitting at the dining room table.

Zachary started saying, "I don't know why you get the last say of what I do and don't do."

Kait started screaming at him, telling him that he was constantly doing things to stress Mom out, sneaking out of the house, smoking, etc.

Zach pushed his burrito to the side and said, "I'm not hungry, you can have this."

He ran back upstairs and slammed the door again. Lincoln walked upstairs and went in his bedroom, which was directly across the hall from Zachary's room. He turned on Fortnite. A few minutes later, he heard Kait calling Zachary to come back down and eat his dinner. She called him several times, but Zachary never answered her.

So, Lincoln walked across the hall and knocked on his brother's door, "Zach, Kait is calling you to go downstairs and eat." Zach never replied. He knocked several times, even put his ear up to the door to listen, but didn't hear anything. He ran downstairs into the kitchen and grabbed a spoon.

Kait saw him grabbing the spoon. "What are you doing, Link?"

126

"Zach isn't answering the door, I tried opening it, but it's locked, and you're calling him, so I'm going to go upstairs and unlock the door with a spoon."

They both ran upstairs. Lincoln took the spoon and twisted the lock open. They had to push the door open together because there was stuff in the way. They walked in the room, but neither of them saw Zachary. Lincoln looked to his left and saw his brother dangling in his closet. He got scared and quickly ran back downstairs, not knowing what was happening. He thought Zachary was playing some kind of joke to scare them. When he heard Kait screaming, he became terrified. He started screaming and crying, not knowing what was happening or what to do.

From that point, Kait told me a little about the events that took place after Lincoln left the room. She tried for ten minutes to get her brother down. She tried finding a knife or anything sharp to cut him down, but couldn't find anything. Finally, she called me. Right after I hung up the phone, Jonathan's ex-wife and her husband showed up. Kait begged the husband to go upstairs and get him down, but he said he couldn't. Kait was so angry with him for quite a while. She struggled with the "what if" he could have gotten him down. She would not talk to me about the events that took place other than that.

It took her a really long time to walk me step-by-step through the events from her perspective. The one detail that fucked me up when I heard everything from her perspective was the fact that she said, "When I first touched his body, his t-shirt was warm and clammy, Mom, what if I could have been strong enough to get him down? His body was warm!" I always knew that it couldn't have been too long after he had made that choice from when they found him, but this confirmed it, and my heart once again was shattered for all three of my children. My poor Kait was truly struggling with her pain in silence all of this time, and proceeded to tell me that she just couldn't get the image of him out of her mind.

Kaitlynn and Lincoln were going through motions, trying to adapt to this new life without their brother. I immediately enrolled the three of us in counseling sessions, and we each saw a counselor consistently for the whole year following Zachary's death.

Kait pushed herself back into her usual routine- school, volleyball, home, repeat. I was really grateful for volleyball because that was the only outlet she seemed to take comfort in. Other than that, I began to notice her isolating herself from the world and sleeping her pain away.

Although he was only six, Lincoln had his struggles too. If Kait was in her bedroom with the door closed, he would constantly go up to the door and say, "Kait, are you good?" You could tell that the whole experience had him worrying about us a whole lot more. Death was now a reality in his innocent mind. A reality that separated him from someone he loved.

We all had our struggles for sure, but never could I have imagined the struggles that I had yet to face.

Chapter 21

It's Time to Move On

I had to go back to work three days after his funeral. I'm not sure what they expected of me, but I was still under a probationary period and wasn't supposed to miss any time at all, I was literally a walking zombie. I was also a single mother, and I knew I couldn't survive without a job. I had no choice but to go back!

When you lose somebody you love, people huddle around you for a bit. They try to comfort you by saying and doing all kinds of things. They bring you food, run errands for you, they try to be helpful, but they're not in your shoes, so they can never truly understand the exact pain you're feeling. Maybe they lost a parent, maybe they lost a friend or family member, maybe they even lost a spouse or a child. Whoever they lost, it really doesn't matter in that moment to you because it wasn't the person you lost. So deep down, you shake your head as you're listening to their words or receive their actions. They can't possibly know how *I* am feeling.

The age-old "it's time to move on" played in my head. But who really gets to decide when it is that time for me? It doesn't matter how many people tell you it has come to that time when you're living through it; you accept that there's not an actual time where you feel you have moved on. Life as you know it has ended, there's no returning to it, so where in the world are you supposed to "move on" to?

Two weeks before the 16ᵗʰ of every month, I would panic, every day, thinking about the 16ᵗʰ of the month approaching. I would count the days that he had been away from me. And on the actual 16ᵗʰ, forget it! I was a wreck! I would fall to my knees and cry uncontrollably. The 16ᵗʰ became a haunting number to me. Every month, it was a horrible reminder of everything I had lost on the 16ᵗʰ of September.

Then there were the sirens. It didn't matter whether I was driving, at work, or at home. If I heard a siren, it was an instant trigger, and within seconds I was back at the scene. The panic attack would cripple my body. My face would go numb, and my fingers would cripple inward due to lack of oxygen. The doctor prescribed me medication to help me, but it wasn't just the sirens.

I was going through all the motions to keep on track with "life as usual," but there was no life left in me. I was literally having at least 5 to 6 severe panic attacks a day. I didn't even have a clue what would trigger some of them. I would be sitting at work, and suddenly I'd start replaying all the events of that day. I would have to leave my desk and go to a dark room because I would begin to hyperventilate.

It eventually got to the point where I lost all concentration. I couldn't keep my thoughts straight. Nothing in my life felt okay. One of the most difficult times through this darkness was the actual concept of time. My days would draaaaaag on for eternities. I had literally lost ALL concept of time. I'd look at the clock at 8:05 and would think an hour went by, but when I looked again, it would be 8:07. Minutes felt like hours, no exaggeration. By the time I left work each day, I was exhausted.

I still had two kids at home to care for. I felt terrible for my surviving children. I'm sure I was more of a programmed robot than a loving mother during the first few months and probably into the majority of that first year. I could barely get myself up and out of bed, but somehow I managed to ensure they were taken care of as well. Get up, get the kids to school, go to work, feed them, survive, and repeat. Life was no longer about living, it was simply an endless loop.

I forced myself to take Lincoln trick-or-treating. Halloween was only forty-five days after Zachary had left me in this world; left me to take his little brother trick-or-treating. This was supposed to be their thing. Something they did together, and now they never would. My boyfriend and his youngest, Liam, joined us. The boys ran up to ring the doorbell, and I instantly started balling. "Zach always went trick or treating with them, and now he's not here."

My boyfriend asked me to compose myself for the boys. He told me to enjoy Lincoln trick-or-treating.

Without hesitation, I cried, "Fuck you! If your kid was dead, you tell me if you'd compose yourself."

I was so upset. I know now that he meant well, but comments like that were lopped together with all the, "Maybe it's time to move on" comments I was often hearing from people.

Every day I would cry. Every day I would panic. Every day I felt like I had died with Zachary.

I just couldn't find the strength to be productive.

One day, I was at work processing payments. A check that was mailed in had the name Zachary on it. I instantly began to uncontrollably sob at the thought that my kid would never have his name on a checkbook. Then I was taunted by all the important milestones of life he would never experience-graduating high school, getting his driver's license, getting married, having a mother/son dance at his wedding.

We moved into our new farmhouse in November. Shortly after moving, I ended up losing my job for being "unable to perform to their expectations." I was angry that my boss couldn't understand, but I also couldn't blame them. I was unable to keep any sort of thought straight, much less continue managing a full-time job, two traumatized children, and my own mental health. It was too overwhelming. I realized then that unless you have lived through something like this, you won't understand what it is like for the person suffering.

Chapter 22

The Grief & Guilt

If a parent loses their child to death at the hands of a fatal illness or unexpected accident, I'm not sure of the grief and pain they might go through. My child had met death on his own terms through his own hands. I think for that reason alone, the guilt rapidly grew day after day until it consumed me. His happy face would play in my mind over and over. Then, for no reason at all, I'd suddenly picture him in the casket. A lifeless face I didn't recognize.

The guilt physically exhausted me. It was as if I was carrying his dead body around my chest everywhere I went. I blamed myself over and over. I was his mother. I should have known the pain he was living with. I should have seen this coming, but I hadn't. Why hadn't I seen it? What else had I missed? Did I even know my child? It was one accusation after another. I blamed myself over and over.

The first month that I lost my job, I would get up, take the kids to school, come home, and sleep all day. On days that I wasn't sleeping, I was browsing through Zachary's phone and social media. I would fall apart at every picture, every video, every post. I literally would just cry. How could I have missed the pain?

Zachary's social media would haunt me. He had shielded me from his pain. Never could I have imagined the pain he was going through, the bullying he was receiving from the rumors, and the internal torment he struggled with. For months prior to his death, he made comments on Snapchat, putting them out there for the world to see. He'd post things like, "Somebody talk to me before I kill myself." "I'm so fucking depressed."

I never knew. Zachary was never diagnosed with depression. He was a super "happy" kid! Always smiling, always laughing.

I developed an unhealthy obsession with his Snapchat. I started reading through every single message that he sent and discovered that from April 2018-September 2018, when he took his life, he was telling kids about how sad, depressed, and unworthy of living he felt. He told kids repeatedly that he wanted to kill himself. He was crying out for help almost every day, but never once told me how he was feeling. Why hadn't I noticed? Even if I had paid more attention, would I have believed it?

What blew my mind even more than his post were the reactions of kids. They never responded with legitimate concern. It was as if they thought he was like the boy who cried wolf. Was that really what society had become? Kids were so used to their friends posting that they were depressed or suicidal to the point they no longer believed something might actually happen?

Yes, there were some that showed him they cared or told him that he mattered. But the majority seemed to brush off his words without a thought. It broke my heart! There were a ton of kids who were cutting themselves. They were pretty open about it in their chats. Zach ALWAYS listened to them, and always did what he could to talk his friends out of harming themselves.

However, at the hospital, on the night of his death as they stripped his clothes off him, and I noticed that he had been cutting his own thighs. It devastated me to see fresh cuts along with scars on his inner thighs, I assume he chose that area of his body to hide it from me. He never wanted to worry me.

I had always allowed the kids to talk to me about anything and everything. Zachary was the one that would come to me with all sorts of crazy topics, why had he never mentioned this to me? Why did he decide it was his own burden to bear? As I continued reading the posts- day after day- the guilt consumed me all the more.

I spent so much time playing through every detail of his short teenage life. There was a time that he told me he had felt sad and didn't know why. Was that the moment I missed? Was that his cry for help and I had brushed it off as teenage angst? The "what ifs" and "how could I have missed this" tormented my soul.

Losing someone you love is one thing, trying to live without them is a whole other struggle.

The driven person, the one who seemed to have her life completely together, was gone. She'd been replaced with a hollow shell of the woman she once was. Up to this point, I had been able to control almost every thing in my life- the good and bad! I was able to "fix" things. Abusive relationship? Fixed it by getting a divorce and moving across the country. Second abusive relationship? Fixed it by recognizing I wanted more for myself and my kids. Daughter being sexually abused? Fixed it by contacting the authorities and getting the kids in counseling. I was proud that we were able to move forward and overcome these things as a family.

Financial burdens of single parenthood? Fixed it by becoming a bad ass at my job. I made killer money for a single parent, and was proudly able to provide whatever the kids wanted! I WAS ABLE TO FIX any problem that ever presented itself into my life. But THIS…there was no "fixing" this.

Zach couldn't be brought back. I'd never again be able to see my baby boy. I'd never be able to hold his hand, to hug him, to play with his hair, to kiss him goodnight. He would never again tell me, "I love you, Mom." The realization that all the control I thought I had was simply an illusion devastated me even more. I was an emotional basket case. I really just wanted to die as well. But I had two surviving kids that needed their mom. How would that be fair to them? End my own pain only to cause them further pain? I knew that I had to continue on, but I wasn't even sure where to start.

Chapter 23

The Club Nobody Wants to Join

I'm sure the hollow person I had become was painful to be around. As I said, I had to be let go from work because I could no longer perform the tasks that were required of me. I can't imagine what my co-workers thought. They must have thought I was crazy, maybe some felt sorry for my loss. Who knows?

Then there were the friends and family. They're the people closest to you, so of course, they are going to do their best to help you through your loss. They come around often and do everything they can to help. But at some point, the visits become fewer because, let's just be honest, when you're a hollow person, there's not much there to visit with. When your brain has been reprogrammed with grief and despair, there's not much there to encourage. Aside from that, there's not any type of manual for what to say and what not to say.

"Laura, you have to keep moving forward for Kait and Lincoln."

"You have to get over it and move forward for the kids."

"You still have two kids to live for."

"You still have two kids that need you."

Sure, they meant well, but man, would those words upset me.

Even my boyfriend was trying his best to encourage me. Unfortunately, I wasn't able to see just how much Zachary's death was affecting him as well. He had treated Zach like his own son. He was struggling just as much as I was, but I was oblivious to the pain. He turned to alcohol to drown out the pain. I allowed myself to be so consumed with self-hatred that I broke up with him. There was no way that I deserved to be loved, not that I had anything to give if I did deserve it.

I felt the worst for Lincoln and Kait. While they were at school, I'd spend the entire day crying, when they got home, it was silent tears. Dealing with a broken mother was in no way fair to them, but I had no way to fix it.

I was invited to a mom's grief group. This group was specifically for mothers who have lost a child. It wasn't specific to suicide. There were moms in there who lost a kid to drug over dosage, others to accidents, but the overall common ground was the loss of a child. I sat in the meeting completely numb. I was asked to share my story, then I listened to others share theirs.

I agreed to go to the meeting, looking for hope. These moms had also lost their children. Maybe they could give me hope that one day the weight I was carrying on my chest would be lifted. The knot in my throat that often suffocated me would soon go away. Instead of finding that hope, I found myself amongst even more dark hopelessness. Moms who had lost their children years ago confessed to crying every single night. I heard their pain. But even more, I FELT their pain.

After the meeting, I sat in the parking lot in my car, screaming at the top of my lungs, "WHYYYYY!!!??? WHY DO I HAVE TO BE PART OF A DEAD KID CLUB??? WHY CAN'T I BE A PART OF A COOL MOM GOLF CLUB INSTEAD?"

I gripped the steering wheel until my knuckles turned white, shaking my body back and forth, screaming in agonizing rage and pain. This was not the plan I had made for my life. This was not who I wanted to be.

The group had a private page on Facebook. I blasted my pain on the page, speaking about not wanting to be a part of that club. The group session hadn't helped; it had finalized reality. Zachary was never coming back. This pain was never going away.

Even writing about that night in this moment, two years later, makes my stomach nauseated. I can taste the bitterness and the impending taste of sadness. Yes, sadness has a taste.

Chapter 24

Gabriela, Party of 4...I Mean, 3

There are so many things that happen after your child dies. So many emotions that get bottled up or blown up. I apologized a few chapters back that things might get a little jumbled and timelines might get a little skewed. The thought had crossed my mind to leave some things out altogether, but who would that benefit?

Maybe you purchased this book because you, too, unexpectedly picked up a membership to the Dead Kid Club. I don't say that to be insensitive. I say it like it is because there is no right way to say it. It sucks! Parents burying their children-for whatever reason- is simply fucked up! You might not like my bluntness, you might not like my language, but I guarantee if you've joined the club, you get it.

So, I'm going to continue through the emotions I experienced along the way.

Before Zachary died, dinner was the only time during the week that the kids and I stopped what we were doing and gathered together. Kait and Zachary had a lot of afterschool activities, I worked long hours, so this brief hour gap was our family time;

the calm before the crazy chaotic nightly routine. Kait and Zach were fourteen and sixteen. They had gotten pretty good at inventing new meals and cooking them together. I'd pick up Lincoln from afterschool care and we'd rush home to set the table and eat.

As a mother, you learn to adapt quickly. When I had Kait, it was no longer just "me," I had increased to a party of two. This little human was fully dependent on me, and I knew that I wasn't just an individual person anymore, the dynamic in my brain automatically changed my identity and my mindset. Then, I had Zachary and Lincoln bumping "me" up to a party of 4.

Just like any other routine, there are things that get ingrained in your muscle memory, things that you do without even thinking about it. Your body somewhat goes on auto-pilot. After Zachary died, that's how I set the dinner table. The first time that I managed to make myself cook, I went to set the table and automatically grabbed four forks. When I realized that we only needed three for dinner that night, it shattered me. I managed to set the table for the three of us, but once we sat down for dinner, the heaviness filled the room. The kids quietly ate their food.

No dinner time conversations. No uncontrollable laughter to follow. I took a bite at my first "party of 3" dinner. The empty chair at the table was more than I could bear. It wasn't just me; I could see the same heavy weight in Lincoln and Kaitlynn's eyes as well. We didn't finish dinner that night, I ended up clearing the table and having a panic attack.

From that day forward, the dinner table became cluttered with unopened mail and unpacked boxes. Kait, Lincoln, and I developed a new routine- make a plate and eat in the living room, something I had never allowed in the past. But this was the new me, the Zach-less me. If this allowed me to avoid the empty fourth chair, then so be it.

It took me a year and a half to realize that I was subconsciously preventing myself from enjoying family dinners at the table. We slowly began having family dinners at the table again. I won't say that it was easy, but it was certainly needed.

Chapter 25

Airplanes & Christmas Trees

As I said before, there are a lot of people that give you the "helpful" advice to move on after you've lost a loved one. If I had to look back over the time since Zachary's death and pinpoint a moment as the "moved on" moment, I don't think that I could have. Outliving a child is not something that can be moved on from. The numbness and pain from the loss, mixed together with all the good things that happened. Some of those things mixed like oil and water. I can look back and clearly identify that God was bringing healing to our family through this moment or that one time. But there are other times when everything mixed together like water and milk, causing a cloudy blur. Were things good? Were things bad? Was it two months down the road, twelve weeks, a year? Not quite sure.

The day that we had dinner as a family at the dining room table was one of those moments where it felt like the hollow shell was breaking, and some light was returning to my soul.

Moving into our new farmhouse was certainly another.

Kait had no desire to leave our old house. She found it comforting to be in the house that had so many memories of her brother. I was the complete opposite. The only memory I could picture in that house was Zachary dying. It was painful and horrific. I never wanted to step foot in the house again. Because she was having such a hard time with the move, I asked the owners if I could paint her bedroom the week before we moved in. I wanted to do something special for her.

The five-acre farm we had purchased was really big. It had rows and rows of Christmas trees across the property, somewhere around 1500. For the past thirty years, it had been open to the public every holiday season as a "you cut" Christmas tree farm. I had initially planned to tear down the trees so we could have horses, but as box of chocolate life most usually went, plans changed. One night, I had a dream. Zachary was telling me the farm was fruitful. I decided to continue the farm's Christmas tradition and open the farm to the public to cut their own Christmas trees once more.

We took ownership of the property the Monday before Thanksgiving.

Our holiday traditions had already been altered when Zachary wasn't around to take Lincoln trick-or-treating. Now it was time for Thanksgiving, the first "family get together" holiday without the entire family. Even though I had already decided I didn't want to cook a Thanksgiving dinner, I was conflicted. I felt that my selfishness might be cheating Kait and Lincoln from enjoying their tradition. But I was in a hopelessly dark place, and didn't care too much about traditions.

146

God clearly had a way of watching out for my kids even when I couldn't, because the night before Thanksgiving, we came home and found an entire Thanksgiving feast at our doorstep. I guess that was my sign that I would be continuing my Grandma Lynn's Thanksgiving tradition, whether I wanted to or not. I couldn't tell you if it turned out good or if there were some things I overcooked. To be honest, the only thing on my mind that day was having to face Zachary's empty seat at the dinner table.

However, there was one crystal clear memory about that Thanksgiving that I will never forget. I walked outside to tell the kids dinner was ready, when suddenly, I look up at the sky and noticed a small private airplane circling our farm. Lincoln was running around the farm waving his hands up in the air. Jokingly, I told him to stick his thumb out and see if he could hitch a ride. As if he could really hitchhike on a plane, right?

Around this same time, my chest began filling with sadness. I was about to have a panic attack, I just knew it. And it was all because of that empty chair sitting in the dining room. I focused on the small white airplane circling our property, hoping that it would take my mind off everything bad.

The plane dipped down and landed in the fifty-acre cornfield behind our property. It seemed to be heading toward the back of our property. I told Lincoln to run over to the back of the property and get a better look. It wouldn't bother me a bit if the food inside got cold. The tiny two-seater antique airplane stopped at the back of our property line, and the pilot opened the door. "Hi, I'm your new neighbor. Wanna go for a ride?"

I was so overwhelmed with joy that the heaviness I felt went away, along with the brewing panic attack. The kids got a chance to go up in the plane, and then I got a chance to go up in the plane. Being in the sky was not only peaceful, but it gave me a sense that I was somehow a little bit closer to my son. I got off the plane and thought to myself, "Did that really just happen?" This was like something out of a movie!

Was this our new life? The kind of life where airplanes land in our backyard and take us on rides?

That same week, there was an organization that had heard our story. They showed up with a ton of people to decorate the Christmas tree farm. Hundreds of lights, a sleigh, bows-strangers just came to my aid to help me prep for the Christmas tree sales. Angels on earth!

The Friday after Thanksgiving, people started coming to buy Christmas trees. There was a news story that aired about our Christmas tree farm opening in honor of Zachary. Throughout the next few weeks, people from all over who had lost loved ones to suicide drove specifically to our farm to buy a tree. Many of them shared their story with us. My heart was filled with so much joy. Despite my pain, being around people was exactly what I needed.

Most of the memories of Thanksgiving and Christmas faded into that milky blur. I was still numb, but being around these strangers got me through it.

Chapter 26

Amazing...Grace

When we moved into the farmhouse, it became clear that we had some kind of pipe problem in the upstairs bathroom. The pipes were located just above the kitchen, and we began to see water dripping from the ceiling. I really didn't even want to think about having to replace the pipes. It would cost me thousands of dollars, and I simply didn't have the extra money.

I called a plumber, who, in fact, confirmed that we had a terrible leak and it was going to cost me a ton of money, not only that, but he stated we were going to have to rip out all of the shower tiles so that he could access the pipes behind the shower wall. It first started in one bathroom, so I told the kids we were going to have to stop using that bathroom until I could afford to fix it. And then, of course, the second bathroom started to leak into the kitchen, so I finally broke down and had no choice but to call a plumber again.

Now let me preface this, prior to this, a few months back, I had a dream about Zach. Zachary was with twelve other boys, all of them wearing red shirts with white letters. They were running around the farmhouse in this fast-forward kind of pace. Zach stopped when he saw me watching them, and said, "Oh, hi Mom, don't worry. We are here to fix everything, you don't have to worry at all." At the time, I thought it's just a dream.

The plumber showed up to give me an estimate, but surprisingly said, "Ma'am, there's nothing wrong with your pipes."

The guy must have thought that I'd lost my mind because I turned on the showers, both of them; mind you, the kids and I could physically see the water steadily dripping into our kitchen. Our ceiling had even been damaged from the water. I kept telling the guy, "You're wrong, check again." We let the water from the showers run for forty minutes, and not a single drop. The guy finally said, "I'm sorry, ma'am, I don't see a sign of any leaks. Your pipes are perfectly fine." I called Jonathan and every handy guy I knew to see if maybe they had somehow come in my house and "fixed my pipes," but everyone would chuckle and respond to me by saying, "Umm, nooo." Haha! I dropped to my knees and uncontrollably sobbed with joy and disbelief. Once again, I thought I had lost my mind, but I was seeing this with my own eyes. They weren't just small leaks, they were a steady flow of water where I'd have no choice but to fix them with money I didn't have. It meant more credit card debt. I kept thinking "HOW?" Maybe I had lost my mind, but over and over again, I had witnessed the water leaking from the pipes into the kitchen. I can't explain to you to this day HOW those leaking pipes were fixed, but what I can tell you is that I was overcome by gratitude that made me drop to my knees and thank God. The twelve boys with Zach were vividly in my mind from my dream, running around my farm with tools, and fixing everything.

I grew up Catholic, my family would go to church on special holidays. From as far as I can remember, my grandmother taught me to say my prayers before bedtime, which consisted of the Lord's Prayer. I always thought that I had to be some kind of "perfect" person to gain access to the kingdom of heaven. These crazy little miracles were beginning to mess with my mind. First, Zachary telling me about his ride with Kait and Haile the night he died. Then the dream of him fixing the pipes. Was there really a God trying to get my attention? Even more so, was my son really with him?

When I was a child, I saw God kind of like a magic Genie in a lamp. I would pray because prayer was instilled in me as a child. But these prayers were always about "wishes" I needed granted. I didn't understand Christianity. I had no idea I could actually have a relationship with Christ. Despite the supernatural moments, I still had the heaviness taunting me.

I couldn't bear this pain anymore... it was too much. I began to have my own thoughts of suicide. I wanted to join my son, but didn't know how I could ever leave Lincoln and Kaitlynn with this pain. I walked into church the weekend after Easter. I had literally hit rock bottom. The pastor stood up and said, "The enemy will try to destroy you, he will steal your joy...you'll have a loved one taken from you...you'll find yourself in a broken relationship...you'll find that you've lost a job." Those words resonated with me. They touched deep into my soul because I was living out every single one of them. I was at my worst, and God wanted me? That's what His grace was all about? Saving a wreck like me from the darkness that had consumed my soul?

What an amazing revelation! I began to read Scripture, and I built a relationship with Christ. The relationship I was building, more than anything else, was what pulled me from the darkness and comforted my soul. It saved me!

"God blesses those who mourn, for they will be comforted" (Matthew 5:4 NIV).

Chapter 27

Jesus, Take the Wheel

Everyone lives out a different story. I don't care how similar ours might be. We each have to make our own decisions and stand by them. Although many people warned me of the toxicity of my marriage, it was ultimately I who had to make the decision to let go of what I thought was love. In the same way, no one could ever tell me how to navigate through the pain I experienced after losing my son. And I couldn't even begin to tell someone else how to navigate through their own pain. The only thing I do know and will stand by over and over and over is the healing love of God. As you can probably tell throughout the story you've read so far, I'm not some holy roller. I don't have it all together.

The amazing thing that I have learned is that God doesn't ask us to have it all together. There are so many stories in the Bible about Jesus spending time with the broken people of His day. I was that broken person even before I lost Zachary, I just didn't realize it. I had all my priorities so mixed up and backwards. Work was my driving force, money was vital to existence, and my kids took a backburner to long hours at the office. Losing Zachary broke all that I was, destroyed me from the inside out. But the amazing thing is that God took hold of all that brokenness and called it His own. He made beautiful things out of the darkness.

I can't even begin to explain all that God has done for me, even in moments I didn't realize He was at work. But one thing I can confirm is the healing He has orchestrated in my life.

There came a point, sometime after Zachary's death, where I remember driving home from my boyfriend's house. We had already broken up, and I honestly don't even remember why I went over there. As I was speeding home, I could feel a panic attack coming on. I literally began slapping myself in the face and screaming. Somehow, I made it to my driveway and dragged myself into my house. In the midst of panic and uncontrollably crying, I fell to my knees and said, "I can't do this! God, if you're real, if you exist, take the wheel because I just can't anymore. I screamed, "TAKE IT, TAKE THE WHEEL, I DON'T WANT IT."

I took my anti-anxiety meds, my depression pill, and prayed the Lord's Prayer. I cried and begged for God to please let me feel my son's peace. I couldn't handle anything anymore. I needed Zachary. I needed to know that he was okay. I needed to hear his voice.

I absolutely couldn't take the physical weight that I was carrying on my chest anymore. I prayed that God would take me.

Then one night, I went to a benefit dinner for my boyfriend's cousin, who had died the same day as Zachary. The dinner was held an hour and a half away from where we lived. However, when we arrived, we were "randomly" seated at this table with an older couple who had lost their son years ago. You'll find out in a moment why I say "randomly".

They shared their story with us. The loss had affected their daughter quite significantly. She decided to become a crisis counselor. Their daughter happened to be the crisis counselor who was called to aid the kids at Zachary's school after his suicide. I was blown away; what were the odds of that? Complete strangers from another town had heard the story of my son. And on top of that, their family had been affected by the loss of a child, and they were able to provide a message of hope.

On the way home from the dinner, I was driving, and my boyfriend was in the passenger seat of the car. Suddenly, while driving, I began to picture Zachary opening and closing doors frantically as if he was looking for us in our old house where he had passed away. The house had only been occupied by our packed boxes and furniture thirty days now. I had not been back there since his death. But I had this terrible anxiety from the vision. I told my boyfriend, "I have to go to the house right now to pray for Zachary."

It was around 11 PM, and he asked, "Right now?"

I said, "YES!" and told him what I was envisioning. I drove us to the house. The moment I pulled into the driveway, I began to panic and cry. I forced myself to walk into the house and head upstairs, all the while having flashbacks of the day when he died.

157

As I approached the stairs, I could see the paramedics bringing him down in the stretcher. I took one step at a time, my feet felt heavy, and my soul broken. I finally made it to the second floor. I walked into his bedroom, and I felt stiff, cold, and in shock. All I could do was stare at his empty closet in panic. I began to pray, and suddenly, my boyfriend says to me, "Stop looking at the closet."

He pulled me close to comfort me. We sat on Zachary's black futon, and I continued to cry and pray as Jonathan held me. Then I heard Zach's voice again… "Mom, Mom, Mom, please listen, God is only letting me do this one time."

"I've lost my damn mind again. I can hear Zach."

It was as if he was speaking to me telepathically, just like the night he died. "No, Mom, it's me, listen. God is only letting me do this one time, please, you have to listen. I need you to feel my peace. It's really me, Mom, you're not crazy, just feel my peace."

In that moment, I felt my son's arms wrap around me like a warm blanket on the harshest winter night. The weight I had been carrying around since his death was physically lifted off my chest. I felt my son, and I felt his peace. Tears stopped rolling down my face; everything stopped as if we stood together in silence holding each other, and then he said, "I love you, Mom." Since that day, I haven't heard his voice again, but despite the darkness and pain I carry, I am comforted by the peace he wanted me to feel. It was as if my son literally knew I was carrying that physical heaviness, and he had begged God, along with me, to just let me feel his peace so that I knew he was okay.

Does it still hurt not having my son here with me on earth? Absolutely! It hurts like hell. I would give anything in the world to have him here. But in that moment, the weight from the guilt and grief slowly begin to subside.

Chapter 28

Out of the Ashes

I missed a lot of signs with Zachary. He was such a selfless person, and never wanted me to know he was in pain. He kept it to himself when he was around me, but his social media painted a much different picture. Snapchat had post after post, speaking of how depressed he was or how much he wanted to die. Instead of burying myself with guilt, I eventually began using the guilt to fuel me.

I started posting suicide awareness messages on social media, encouraging people to seek help. I also decided to begin posting preventative posts on Zachary's Snapchat. Kids started reaching out to me on his Snapchat. They talked to me about Zach, and shared stories of how he was with other kids at school. They would send me pictures or videos that they had of him.

Then to my surprise, some of them also began talking to me about their own struggles. The conversations would always start about Zach. But they would soon begin to share their feelings, their own depression, and they would open up about their own thoughts of suicide.

Hearing kids open up to me somehow helped me begin to understand how my own son was feeling. It made me realize the struggle life had become for Zachary, and why he eventually made the choice to end his own life. The pressures that the kids in today's day and age have to go through with social media, with bullying, with trying to fit in, having a constant image of "perfection" painted through filters on social media, etc. It's way too much weight for their young hearts and minds to bear.

Society constantly throws images of perfection in their developing mind. Ninety percent of the teens I have spoken to and asked why they want to die, have given me answers like, "Because my clothes don't fit in." "I'm ugly." "No one likes me."

There is a strong desire for acceptance. Unfortunately, even if they are from a loving family or a part of a close friend group, most of them are under the illusion that they will never measure up to the expectations needed to be truly accepted by others.

One of the most useful things I have learned while speaking with these teens is the need to paint a picture of the future. Their feelings are very real. They should be acknowledged and validated. We cannot simply shrug them off as, "What do you have to worry about at this age?" But they absolutely must be shown hope amongst their darkness. When a child is hurting, they are living in the pain they feel RIGHT NOW. They can't see past their current pain. The only way we can truly help them is by painting a picture of the future, such as, "This pain won't last forever. When you graduate high school, you'll find the love of your life and have children of your own." Or, "Just wait until you go to college, you're going to have a blast!"

It's important to let them know that in adulthood, their memories of high school will wear off. They're living in the now, the painful NOW, so we just have to take them to a place they cannot currently picture, and paint a tomorrow.

Because God has had such a significant impact on my life, I will often tell them about God as well. I build an image of a future, but also introduce them to their Creator. "God made you on purpose, for a purpose. Don't ever doubt that or brush that off. He looks at you and sees value in the person you are right now."

I was devastated when I lost my job. It sent me into an even deeper depression. Little did I know through it all God had a bigger purpose. Little did I know he was taking my pain, along with these conversations, and creating something new out of the ashes.

On my farm, there is a huge garage building. After a month of laying around while my children were at school, I finally told myself I had to get up and do something. I'd drop the kids off at school, come home, and spend the ENTIRE day outside in my yard. I would cut the grass around the 1500 Christmas trees and spend time hanging out with the horse. Being in nature felt so good. Despite my darkness, I was beginning to feel as if I was somehow being comforted.

I started to rehab the garage building- ripping out shelves, patching holes, painting. Jonathan would come over every single day after work to paint, trim, and help me out...he knew I now had a vision. I wanted to turn the building into an event venue. As I had noticed at Christmas with the tree sales, surrounding myself with people was super healing. Talking and sharing Zach's story, our story, was like a breath of fresh air.

I ended up obtaining a business license and opening up an event venue. Once we rehabbed the garage building, it was rented out to families for parties, life ceremonies, weddings, and graduations. I was booked solid every single weekend. The venue had me constantly busy, which meant my mind was always occupied. There was no time to lay around and sob anymore, now it was time to get up and rebuild. To get to start knowing the new me.

I kept posting suicide prevention posts on Zachary's Snapchat. I'd post things like, "Your life matters to me, please stay alive- suicide hotline: 1-800-273-8255." Teens continued messaging me. Normally, it would be encouraging things like, "Thank you for caring." Or "Thank you for being strong and posting." But more and more began reaching out with their own struggles with depression and thoughts of suicide. The messages kept coming at all hours of the day and night.

I was so emotionally drained after talking to them, but I never wanted any other mother to feel the pain that I was carrying. So, I continued listening and encouraging. I never wanted to stop doing what I was doing. God had brought me through my son's death, so He could give me the strength to encourage these lives. I began to see the impact that Zachary's story was making in kids, and I started to share more and more. I would watch kids going from being depressed and suicidal, to finding hope and wanting to continue living their lives.

I was overcome by the joy of making a difference in these kids' lives. I knew that as long as they shared with me, I would listen.

Chapter 29

Marshmallow's Moments in Time

I didn't ask for any of this. But that's life, "...you never know what you're gonna get." Kids continued to contact me via Snapchat. They continued to open up about their problems, and I continued to listen. God had given me a new purpose. I hadn't planned any of it; it had essentially "fallen in my lap." I started to play a huge role on suicide prevention and mental health awareness. Our story was helping others. Parents with struggling teens, and even parents who have lost a child to suicide, somehow we would cross paths, and my purpose begin to appear so clear.

I had named the garage building-turned-event venue after Zachary's nickname, which was "Marshmallow," and Moments in Time came from the thought that we should cherish each moment in time with our loved ones as we never know when our last moment in time together will be. As I mentioned earlier, Marshmallow's Moments in Time was a fairly popular venue. They say the devil will try to steal your joy, well, I had neighbors that went to the county and filed a complaint about "noise." The county shut me down, and I've been fighting for almost a year now to re-open it.

We all have a God-given purpose, and had you asked me what my mine was 22 months ago, I would have never imagined this journey. Through the tragedy of losing my son, my purpose was beginning to seem so clear; through my grief, I was being aligned for my God-given purpose and didn't even know it.

I had accidentally became a Christmas tree farmer. Then through my venue, as I met more and more people and shared our story, I begin to understand that this was no longer just about me. It was much bigger than me. My purpose is to help prevent others from feeling my pain. Through renting out the venue to random strangers, I begin to meet countless people in my community in very similar situations that I'd been faced with in my own life.

God was providing my every need to open doors for me to step up and help others. I was able to use funds generated through the venue to aid kids, like my son, in my community who feel that life is not worth living. I joined the cause to help break the stigma that surrounds mental illness and suicide. I learned quickly that suicide does not discriminate. It doesn't see finances or color; it is the cause of a mental illness that lies to people and makes them believe that everyone around them would be better off if they were dead. It can happen to anyone! It happened to me! My precious son is gone, forever, and that is pain that I would never want anyone else to feel.

And so it is clear, 22 months into my journey, as I write today to share our story, I now know my God-given purpose.

My farm will be a place for people to build long-lasting memories of their moments in time, and help me fulfill my purpose of aiding others.

The venue is currently shut down due to the neighbors' complaints; I am still fighting to reopen it, the fight isn't over, but I only share this part of my story because it's a HUGE part of my story of grace. Every single obstacle that has been put in my way to re-open, God literally has "moved mountains," and continuously shows me that nothing will stand in the way of the purpose that He has for you. In order for the county to even consider me reopening, they demanded that I have "maintenance done" on my property. When I got estimates on the repairs that the county requested, I discovered it was going to cost more than what I make in a year.

I felt defeated. Here I was saying God had given me this purpose, but I had no way to keep it open. Maybe it was time to accept that this brief moment in my life was over. I couldn't afford the repairs, so I'd had to step away from the venue.

Thankfully, God had other plans! A guy who read our story on social media, a random stranger, came to my property to speak to me. He told me God had been so good to him. He just wanted to pay it forward and literally made the repairs to my property that were needed without charging me a penny!

All my life, I had planned and progressed. I did things my way, and while I got places here and there, I never truly felt like I had arrived anywhere. Here I was, throwing my hands up in surrender

169

to God, and He was making things happen that I never- in my wildest dreams- could have imagined would be possible.

Every single time that I am presented with another "speed bump" to slow me down, He allows me to slowly drive over the bumps and allows me to overcome all obstacles thrown in my way. I've had contractors show up on my property on multiple occasions that have unknowingly come to my aid. When I proceeded to talk to them, they admitted to me that they had an urging of the Holy Spirit to help me. There were discounted rates or free labor that didn't even make sense to me. But that's the thing, grace doesn't make sense. I am a testimony of this! Marshmallow's Moments in Time is a testimony of this! He continues to open doors, and miracle after miracle happens when I least expect it.

Chapter 30

I Know the Plans

There's a story in the Bible found in the Old Testament book of Genesis about a man named Joseph. I'm not a preacher by any means, so I'm not going to get into all the details, but Joseph was a man that received a "melted box of chocolates." He went through some terrible things. Yet he came out of them, and had this to say:

"You intended to harm me, but God intended it for good to accomplish what is now being done, the saving of many lives" (Genesis 50:20 NIV).

That is exactly how I feel about my own life. There have been so many things intended to harm me, but God took all that crap, knowing that it would be used for what is being done now- the saving of many lives.

I have encountered tons of parents who have lost a child. Some recently and others years ago, a lot of them are consumed with grief. There are moms I have met who have lost their child decades ago and still can't manage to get out of bed. For years, they have sadly just "existed" in life, and they count the days that they can be with their child again. I can tell you that losing a child, in general, is traumatic, and it's not the way the life cycle is supposed to work. Parents shouldn't ever outlive their children – it's too painful. Losing a child to suicide leaves you not only with the pain of losing your baby, but guilt, unanswered questions, trauma, depression, anxiety, and PTSD. I often wonder how I can get out of bed being only twenty-two months into this journey.

One huge difference that I've noticed between parents who are able to "live" after that life has been taken from them and those that remain in the hollow shell phase is where they place God. It is very normal to blame God for your child's death. I can't tell you how to feel or how to cope, I can only speak from personal experience that I never felt anger towards God in this. Did I think it was unfair to outlive my child? Yes. But I never blamed Him for my child's death. Instead, I pleaded for His comfort. And once I asked Him to take the wheel, my grief began to change.

I found comfort and love in leaning on God to provide all of my needs. Even as a single mother without a job -I would suddenly receive a random check in the mail of an "overpayment" that I made to a utility company from years ago, hundreds of dollars at that! Or an "underpayment" from a previous employer who "shorted me" on a commission check two years prior that I had no knowledge of ever being shorted – but when I called the employer it was a "valid" check. Not chump change, a few thousand dollars to help me cover bills until the next month!

Honestly, just random financial miracles in my time of need that made no sense – He provided! No other explanation!

I have learned that we do not have to be perfect at all. In fact, it is okay to not be okay and to be far from perfect. All we have to do is believe, and once we accept Him as our Lord and Savior, our lives will begin to change in unimaginable ways.

I look back on my life with so much sadness. I was young and in love, but I honestly had no idea what love truly was. Love is what reaches down, scoops up all the broken pieces, and says, "Laura, you are beautiful. You have purpose. I will call you Mine and use you for My purpose. My plans for you are more than you could ever imagine for yourself. Will you let me love you? Will you trust me to take the wheel instead of jerking yourself all over the road?"

God knew the whole entire time. He knew before I was even born where I would be in this very moment twenty-two months after Zachary took his own life.

I had SO many plans for myself. I wanted a family of my own SO badly that I allowed myself to overlook way too many red flags. I dismissed all the gut feelings telling me to break the unhealthy cycle. I allowed myself to be belittled, talked down to, and hit, all in the name of love. That was not and is not love. Domestic violence is very real. When you're in the midst of it, you lie to yourself so much that you begin to believe the lies. "That will be the last time." "Things will be better." "It was my own fault because I…" "One day the person I love will come back."

173

It is ok to have hope. There are relationships that have been restored. But the best thing for you to do is have that hope AWAY from the abuse. My children might have been spared from so many things if I had stood up and said, "You know what, I want to fight for us, but I'm going to do it over here where it is safer and less toxic." I hate that it took me so long to realize the damage I was causing them by staying. I also hate to say it, but throughout my journey, I've learned that trauma is embedded deep into your subconscious mind, and if it isn't worked through and addressed, it creates problems such as feelings of fear, abandonment, and even self-unworthiness. I often struggle with Zach having his leg broken as an infant and being slapped across the face. I'll never know exactly how that awful day was for my baby boy, but I believe that it embedded those types of feelings into his mind, and well…you know the end result.

I'm not putting blame at all as I believe that the demons of depression led him to believe the lies that his mind told him.

Although Kait seems okay and is still in counseling, I still worry every single day about the struggles she will face in her adult life because of the abuse that she endured. I often encourage her to continue working on her mental health and lean on God for comfort and healing.

As far as Lincoln, I am hoping that through counseling, he will someday process and heal from the terrible details of the day he lost his big brother.

I am grateful for all of the counselors that have helped my children and I along the way, but I am super grateful to God for showing us that we WILL make it!

Since Zachary's death, my life as I knew it is no more. There have been so many surreal moments where God has built my faith in Him along this journey. I could write a whole other book, but these are just a few:

- The detective that took on Kait's sexual abuse case was the same officer that arrested my ex-husband the night that he had beat me. He remembered our family and all we had endured in that moment. He fought with everything that he could to bring our family justice.

- Jonathan's ex-wife not allowing me to go upstairs the night Zach died made me really upset. But looking back, I thank God over and over that she wouldn't allow me to see my son. God knew I didn't need to see him like that. I will also forever be grateful of the help she provided Kait in that moment.

- While at Jonathan's grandson's gender reveal party, we ran into one of the nurses in the emergency room who had tried bringing Zach back to life. The baby was named Adrian Zachary.

- Remember the government job, the one where I thought I'd retire from but lost? There was a lady that also worked there two floors above me. The Suicide Prevention walk that my job was sponsoring, the one that my family and I attended just the day before Zachary passed-that walk was for her personal foundation. Four years before I lost my son to suicide, her 19-year-old son had also died by suicide. Here we were, two strangers who never met each other a day before this tragedy, and yet God placed me at that job, so that she could literally take me under her wing, per se, and walk me through the beginning stages of my own grief and pain.

- Being a single mom made it super impossible for the kids and me to ever get one-on-one time together… it was always the four of us, it just so happened that after the walk, Lincoln decided to go with my boyfriend, and Kait was with her friend, so Zachary and I got to go to Beef-a-Roo together. Just the two of us…that was the very last meal I had with my son, and it was so full of laughter, looking back now by design, an amazing and rare opportunity.

- Then, on the one-year anniversary of Zach's death, my siblings had come to visit, and we decided to go to church. The guest speaker began telling a story about his neighbor and best friend, struggling with substance abuse. The man eventually died by suicide. We were all sobbing as if he had chosen the story specifically for us. When we met him after the service, he explained that he hadn't planned to talk about any of that. While he was praying before service, he had been compelled to share the story and speak on Jeremiah 29:11- which was Zachary's favorite Scripture.

- Not only that, but on the weekend of my birthday, the first birthday without my son, I was fighting severe anxiety and depression. It wasn't fair that I was getting to be one year older, and Zachary was not; I was struggling with never feeling joy again without my son here with me. Anyway, the same pastor happened to just be speaking at our church, and to my surprise, when he walked in, he was wearing black jeans and a red and black plaid shirt, Zachary's absolute favorite outfit. My kid wore that at least once a week, if not more! He loved that red and black plaid shirt. Anyway, the pastor said he had a prayer, and of course, it was about depression and anxiety and FINDING JOY again. My son's presence is around me all the time, but that night was as if I was watching my son up on stage, saying, "Mom, it's okay, get rid of the guilt and find joy in life."

- The mom's club that I hated being a part of and sent me into immediate panic was being used as encouragement. Those ladies in that group are people that have helped pick me up when I least expect it. Remember the lady at the suicide walk when I expressed to Zach that I'd be as devastated as she was if anything happened to him? That lady turned out to be one of the moms in the grief group. Her son attended my son's school, and she and I leaned on each other for hope and encouragement.

- The feeling of the last hug…as sad as it makes me, that WAS the last hug I ever gave my son. But I love the fact that we both conveyed how much we loved each other.

- In the midst of my despair, a lady in Alabama who saw a post that I had made on a private group on social media related to my pain, as she, too, had lost her young boy to suicide, and on one of my darkest days, a perfect stranger shared her pain with me, but even bigger than that, she had her best friend draw a portrait of my child for me.

- The pilot that randomly flew down on Thanksgiving to give us rides, turns out he's not just a neighbor, he is a man who experienced the loss of his own child; we share that pain and he has been a huge part of my healing. On several occasions, when I was in the midst of my darkness, he'd just fly down to my backyard and take me flying.

- This book! I had no intentions of publishing a book, and through sharing my story with a random stranger, who reached out to me because they needed my assistance on coming up with what to write for an online suicide prevention carousel, our encounter spiraled into this journey. Again, not part of my plans.

- Jonathan and I broke up for a few months, so part of the story may be confusing as to when we were a couple and were not. Looking back, however, during my darkest times I was not healthy enough mentally to be around anyone! The weekend after Easter, I invited him and his kids to come to church. For a couple of months, he came every weekend, sat next to me, we wouldn't say much to each other at all, but I began to notice HUGE changes within Jonathan, one of them was no longer drinking to self-medicate. This man was literally transformed before my eyes. God needed us to be apart to work on our own healing so that we could be healthy for one another.

Looking back, it has been no coincidence the people I have come in contact with and the paths that have crossed my own. It has been by a much bigger design.

"For I know the plans I have for you,"
declares the Lord, "plans to prosper you and
not to harm you, plans to give you hope and
a future" (Jeremiah 29:11 NIV).

Chapter 31

Fuel the Fire

What a crazy journey this has been! I never imagined how this book might turn out as I began writing down my story. My only focus had been on Zachary's pain and suicide. I knew that I had to get the story out for more people to hear so more people could be aware and more lives could be saved. I had no plans to go all the way back to the beginning of my own life and share the pain I had endured. I didn't intend to share how lost in the darkness I was, but God always knows what He is doing!

Maybe you picked up this book and you are in an abusive relationship.

Maybe you can relate to some of the events that I described, the shred of hope for a better life that has you returning to the abuse over and over. Or maybe, the fear of being a single parent. Maybe it is even simply the fear of failure, you've had so many people tell you the relationship was toxic, and you ignored them. Admitting they were right seems almost painful to accept. Whoever you are and wherever you are at, I urge you to find a mirror and tell that person they are a priceless individual. The person in the mirror deserves more than the abuse they are enduring. The person in the mirror is more than any of their failures or regrets. It is time for that person in the mirror to choose life for themselves. Enduring physical and/or mental abuse is not living, it is barely even existing. Tell that person in the mirror that they deserve much more than they have settled for. That person is beautiful, that person is intelligent, that person has a future that doesn't involve this abuse. If that person in the mirror is you, you are the only one who can decide to change things. But there are those who are willing to help you when you are ready for that change.

You can contact the **Domestic Violence Hotline at 1-800-799-7233. Or, if you cannot safely speak, text the word LOVE to 1-866-331-9474.**

Maybe you picked up this book, and you're the parent of a child who has been sexually abused, or you're that child that was sexually assaulted.

If either of those are the case, I am terribly sorry. There is so much guilt that comes with this. As a parent, it is extremely sad knowing that you weren't able to protect your baby. And as a victim, there is also guilt that comes along with it, but to both parent and victim, please know that this was not your fault. You did nothing wrong; you weren't aware. It is no one's fault except the abuser.

There are services out there that are free for victims of sexual assault and family members of sexually assaulted children that will provide confidential support for you and your loved ones so that you can begin the healing process. The **National Sexual Assault Hotline 1-800-656- HOPE (4673**); they can refer you to local sexual assault service providers in your area.

Maybe you picked up this book because you've lost a child.

You can relate to the pain and agony that I have described. You've experienced, firsthand, the depression that keeps you in bed, unwilling to continue on with life; the empty feeling of knowing that you'll never hug your child again here on this earth. There are support groups that you can attend with other grieving parents. You can visit **WWW.NAMI.ORG** to find support groups in your area. Please feel free to email me as well: **losttodarknesshelp@gmail.com**, and I will get you in contact with any resources that I have available, and provide you with support to help get you through this. Other than that, I'm really not sure of additional help that can be found, here on earth, to heal the emptiness of your soul.

However, if you're willing to seek help outside of this world, there is a God who can transform your sorrow into an unspeakable joy. He can turn your unrest into a peace that is unspeakably indescribable. Accepting Jesus Christ as your Savior will 100 percent transform your life, take away your pain, and guide you to your purpose.

I say this out of my own personal experience. No matter how much of a screw-up I think I am, He is always right by my side despite my imperfections. I handed the wheel over to Him when

I thought I couldn't drive anymore, and I'm so glad I did. He has taken me down roads I never knew existed. He has given me a peace and joy that I never would have thought I could experience again.

Lastly, I imagine there will be someone reading this book who may be struggling with mental illness or who knows someone struggling with depression or suicidal thoughts.

My advice to you is be vigilant! If your friend or family member is constantly telling people they are depressed, don't brush it off as a phase or take it lightly. Ignoring them would be like coming upon someone treading water, saying they were about to drown. Sure, they may seem like they are treading water fine at the moment, but eventually they will tire of the struggle and drown. Don't let this happen! Don't ignore them. If you don't know where the lifesaver is located so you can throw it to them, find someone who does. Meaning, if you aren't sure how to help them, reach out to people who can. Seek out the assistance of a parent, a school counselor, a family counselor, or anybody you trust. Contact the **Suicide Hotline** at **1-800-273-8255 or text 741741**. You can even contact me via **Snapchat** at **Shadow313zc**.

Depression is not a normal feeling that will simply go away like hunger pains. Often times, there are reasons behind why a person is feeling depressed. Counseling can help people get to the root cause of why they are feeling depressed. Others experience depression because of imbalances in their body. Taking antidepressants can help them. Having to take medication does not make someone weak or inadequate, it simply means that something is off inside their body and they need help to rebalance it.

The biggest thing of all is to have people around you. People don't usually wake up one morning and decide to die by suicide. There are often many little signs that go unnoticed. Mood swings or isolation can be signs that something is wrong. I dismissed Zachary's mood swings as a result of puberty. While I don't want you to think that every moody teen is suicidal, I do want you to take notice of when and why they are experiencing these mood swings. Drug use and self-harm, or cutting, are often used to mask the pain that is being felt. If someone you know starts using drugs or harming themselves, do not overlook these things. There is something else lurking just below the surface, something that they are struggling with.

If you're the one struggling, please know that you never have to suffer in this pain alone. There are people that love you. There is help! People DO CARE in spite of what your mind is telling you. I'll say it again, YOU ARE LOVED! Please, please talk about it! Don't go through this darkness alone. Please find hope in knowing that the pain you're feeling will end, and you can live out a full life!

My biggest fear when I began writing this book was wondering what people might think about the choices I had made throughout my life. Then the fear of people thinking I was crazy had crossed my mind at some point. Who wouldn't think I was crazy for claiming to hear my son talk to me from beyond the grave? Even I had my moments where I thought I might be crazy.

But somewhere along the journey, that fear melted away, and the words began to flow over and over. This story was about my life, but it wasn't my story to tell- it belonged to the One who had given me my life- God. My prayer is that He uses something within these pages to speak to you personally and touch your heart so you, too, may be enlightened by grace.